"Michael Neece's *In Kind* is a brave work of enduring optimism that challenges cynicism with empathy, compassion, and self-awareness. Neece takes the world as it is and provides a narrative that helps readers envision a kinder way to navigate it, using his strong conscience and extensive exploration of self as a guide. The tangible takeaways and illuminating exercises in each chapter will empower readers to build powerful connections, foster cultures of empathy, and become catalysts for positive change as they bring more kindness to the world, starting with themselves."

Kristen Hadeed,
author of *Permission to Screw Up*

"*In Kind: Consciously Craft a Meaningful Life and Career* delves into effective networking and mentorship strategies, making it a unique perspective on using kindness to solve challenging interpersonal issues and establish a positive professional reputation. This is a great read for anyone looking to break through the noise and distractions of the workplace to emerge as a respected leader who values meaningful relationships."

Kipp Spanbauer,
Data Scientist and Leadership Advocate

"*In Kind: Consciously Create a Meaningful Life and Career* offers a beacon of hope and a guidebook for a brighter tomorrow. Michael G. Neece takes us on a journey into the heart of kindness and its transformative power to reshape our world. Through captivating stories and real-life examples, he illustrates how kindness can mend broken bonds, heal wounds, and bridge the gaps that separate us. This thought-provoking exploration of kindness doesn't restrict itself to individual actions; instead, it describes how those individual efforts naturally combine to help us build the future we want to live in.

"More than just a book, it's a call to action, an invitation to transform your work environment into something brighter and more harmonious. Learn to implement this vision of a kinder tomorrow and discover the limitless possibilities that await in the pages of this heartwarming and empowering book."

Eyerusalem Fikru Mengistu,
Economist

"*In Kind* is a powerful and transformative book that has changed my ways of approaching people. There are practical, thoughtful, and actionable insights on how leading with kindness can unlock numerous opportunities for growth and success. It has helped me build stronger, trusting relationships at work and in my personal life."

Ishita Shah,
Pharmaceutical Industry Leader

"We've all heard it before, 'Be Kind' or 'Be Nice'. But what does this mean? And why is this important? Learn how to infuse and build kindness in your life and how kindness can positively impact your work life and satisfaction. Take a trip into the compassionate and thoughtful teachings of Michael Neece. In Michael's book *In Kind*, you will navigate through the tools and means to develop the most authentic and meaningful relationships, understand and repair alliances, and find your best self in your relationships with your co-workers and management. Do you want to know more on how to realize this ideal workplace? Grab a copy of this book and let it be your compass to a kinder and more humane life. Enjoy the trip and don't be surprised if you want to take this literary trek more than once."

Tracy Ross,
Quality Assurance Professional

IN KIND

Consciously Craft a Meaningful Life and Career

MICHAEL G. NEECE

KINDNESS

OUR FUTURE IS KIND

BUILD THE FUTURE YOU WANT TO LIVE IN

In Kind: Consciously Craft a Meaningful Life and Career

Cover Design by Robin Locke Monda

Publishing Consultant
Birthabook.com

ISBN: 979-8-9890711-0-4

Published by Our Future Is Kind

Visit www.michaelgneece.com
for additional resources.

To Kate, my compass of kindness, and
Thomas, Sarah, and Ivy, the stars that light my way.

For my parents, who live every moment
with integrity and kindness, and my sister, Brenda,
whose creative energy and deep curiosity inspire me.

This book is also dedicated to the mentors, colleagues, friends,
and countless others who have kept me company along
the journey of self-discovery and helped bring these words to life.

Together, you are the heart of this book.

CONTENTS

Introduction 1

Chapter 1: Our Big Egos in a Bigger Universe 9

Chapter 2: Surpass Your Limits 27

Chapter 3: Who Am I? 49

Chapter 4: Assembling the Right Crew 65

Chapter 5: Growing at Work 81

Chapter 6: Invisible Forces at Work 107

Chapter 7: When Things Don't Go Well 143

Chapter 8: We Are Stronger Together 175

Chapter 9: We Build the Future We Want to Live In 193

INTRODUCTION

WHY SHOULD YOU READ THIS BOOK?

Haven't you had a friend who has struggled with work drama? They pull you into their work culture with a story about overheard gossip tearing the office apart, an arrogant coworker who takes credit for others' work, or the micromanaging supervisor who wastes everyone's time asking for proof that they aren't wasting time. Maybe your friend feels lost, sad, furious, or emotionally wrecked. They feel they should leave but worry that "out there," they'll find something even worse. They want to get out, but their optimism that things can improve, and people can change, keeps them from doing so. What do you tell them?

Since it is usually easier to show compassion to our friends, I have asked you to imagine their situation first. When you are together, you both have that feeling of belonging, right? You want them to feel validated, heard, seen, and safe. You also have the advantage of seeing their situation from a logical standpoint. You can see your friend and their situation clearly, so you probably give them the validation and feedback they seek.

So, what about you? Imagine the tables are turned, and after you've complained about work, that friend wants to comfort you, validating how you feel unsupported, unseen, or like an outsider. Have you watched employees get bullied during meetings and wondered if you were next? Have you noticed a colleague working long hours without recognition and wondered if working above and beyond in quiet anonymity is the right approach? Have you heard hushed voices fade to silence as you approach and wondered if the office gossipers are talking about you?

Sadly, you and most of your friends have probably experienced way more broken work culture than is good for you. Horror stories pervade our news streams about layoffs conducted by email, supervisors mocking concerns brought to them by workers, and companies mandating policies that feel harsh and confusing.

It could be that broken culture, or something within yourself, that makes you feel unwelcome and like you don't belong. Somewhere along the way, maybe you talked yourself into a career path or stumbled into one, but now you lose sleep, can't focus, or find yourself hoping against hope that you don't have to go to work tomorrow. Maybe you took on the family business out of loyalty because no one else would. Perhaps, someone looked at what you loved to do as a high school student and advised that there's no money in poetry, art, history, or something else they didn't see a future in. Maybe, they took it even further and suggested you focus on becoming, for example, an engineer instead. Whatever the cause, now the lost sleep is real. The what-ifs and if-only-I-hads eat away and add to the sense of being lost. On top of having relationships, paying bills, seeing the dentist, and all the other logistics of life, you now have this sense that how you spend your workday is missing something. You might even feel you are in the wrong place doing the wrong work. Or worse, that people who've seemed to enjoy career success are lying.

According to a 2014 article in the Center for Workplace Mental Health, a survey shows that 23% of workers are formally diagnosed with depression. Could feeling misaligned with your job, something you do 40 hours each week, be a contributing factor? When workers show up to work feeling the effects of depression, the research clearly shows that work becomes more difficult, less productive and less fulfilling; thus a powerful and painful feedback loop exists for many.

This book is about illuminating the sometimes hidden internal and external forces that make us feel like we don't belong. The tools you learn here will help you sidestep those forces, stave them off, or handle them efficiently and keep moving. It is about mastering them so you can wake up each day excited to go to work, ready to reshape your job into what you hope it can be, grow your career and network with high-value experiences and people, and create a secure future by using kindness as your compass.

As you learn to honor your belief in kindness, you will rely on self-awareness to help you evolve into your most authentic, highest self. Along the way, you'll have to make some repairs, open your heart, and uplevel your workplace culture one kind act at a time.

WHY AM I THE PERSON TO WRITE THIS BOOK?

Over the last 35 years, I have worked as a leader in five industries. I got a lot of things wrong in my early days, not for lack of positive intent, but because I didn't know what I didn't know. After some challenging moments in my early career, when I did not like how things went, or how I felt, I decided to learn everything I could to make work something I looked forward to, to make my jobs, and how I performed them, things I could be proud of.

I have always been curious about what makes people tick. When I started in the working world, I wondered what makes a good team, how do good leaders know how to lead, and what motivates people. My natural curiosity led me to a seemingly endless stream of books, podcasts, TED Talks, and conversations with friends, trusted mentors, and experts in social psychology, earning an advanced degree in teaching, and looking inside myself in ways that had previously escaped me.

For the next decade, I dug into social psychology. I read, watched, and listened to everything I could about working relationships. I built multiple teams and mentored junior colleagues. I even created an academy, became its director, and taught young colleagues to be successful in their early careers. I scrubbed through my journals and old work-related emails, looking for clues about connecting successfully with coworkers. I mainly focused on missteps and challenges when correcting course. While my successes have helped inform me, my failures have frequently been more illuminating.

Drawing on my experiences, I have crafted this book and packed it with the best strategies, tips, and tricks I have discovered about how to build community, find trusted mentors, and avoid calamitous situations, all while insisting on using kindness as a compass.

If the COVID-19 pandemic hit just as you were starting in the workforce and you feel lost trying to integrate into work culture (or face-to-face work culture in particular), this book is for you. If you are starting over, switching jobs or careers, and need strategies for healthy integration into your new work community, this book is for you. If your workplace feels dangerous, lacks kindness and empathy, or seems *broken*, this book is for you.

Here, I distill the wisdom I have collected from friends and colleagues, their mistakes and successes, and my research into what makes a workplace kinder. Reflecting on these moments represents only a piece of what's required, the first important step. The rest requires action to repair and grow from moments filled with shame. You will have to build muscles around self-awareness, improving your ability to unpack critical moments that lead to helpful answers on how to move forward. The great news is that you can do this with clear strategies and practices outlined in this book.

Throughout, I share career moments when I felt directionless, lost, scared, and alone and how I got through them. You'll get a front-row seat at some of my career's most shame-filled self-loathing moments, so you can see how I survived them and learned from my shame by transforming it into a sense of belonging. I promise these pages will bring you my authentic experiences across five industries plus decades of lessons learned so you can avoid unnecessary suffering and revel in the bounty of a positive work community that extends well beyond wherever you're currently working.

This book also provides practical strategies and essential tools for finding or creating a community in your workplace, regardless of your role and title. My goal is to help you succeed more easily and to show you the inner workings of my career so that you understand that our struggles are normal. The key to getting through it all is self-reflection and living your beliefs about leading with kindness.

As you read, consider the first rule of success in the workplace:

Be kind to everyone, especially yourself.

By investing in kindness, you will learn how to:

- create authentic connections, converting some colleagues into friends.

- find safe mentors who offer guidance rather than judgment.

- be your authentic self with trusted allies to grow faster and more reliably.

- handle toxic factors in the workplace effectively and protect yourself appropriately.

- identify what feedback has value and use that feedback to grow.

- create a network of supporters, champions, and followers who will naturally think of you and suggest your name when opportunities arise.

By the end of this book, I promise you'll see that treating colleagues, supervisors, and those reporting to you with consistent kindness will unlock doors to opportunities and success. Once you harness the tools and strategies in the following chapters, that success will come more easily as you grow your network, all while experiencing more joy and kindness.

I sincerely hope this book makes a difference for you, giving you the tools and strategies to go from hesitation, uncertainty, and dread to a feeling of calm, optimistic confidence that makes it much easier to be kind.

CHAPTER 1

OUR BIG EGOS IN A BIGGER UNIVERSE

Imagine that you have a powerful kindness practice that enables you to create authentic connections at work. You build your network easily, find trustworthy mentors, and bond with champions who speak your name in opportunity-filled rooms. This kind-hearted work community comforts those in pain and deters those who engage in destructive behavior. The workplace feels comfortable and happy, with colleagues celebrating each other even while the work gets done. With mindful consideration of your colleagues, a healthy environment is possible. I can help you get there if you're willing to be brave, honest, and self-reflecting.

Before we dig in, I need you to help me keep this fire burning, if only in your imagination at first. Imagine a work world with more people looking out for each other, everybody hoping for the success of their colleagues, and zero tolerance policy for bullying and unkind behavior. More powerful still, those who feel the need to bully encounter kindness at every turn, so they lay down their harsh tactics and align with the new norm of goodwill. Compassion at work spills into life, and thoughtful, sweet acts at work lead to more listening and support at home and in public. Flash forward a few years, and corporate greed becomes a thing of the past because unhappy executives, who used to fear that others' gains translate into personal losses, realize instead that they have enough, that *they* are enough.

Let's keep going, shall we? Imagine the millions of small kindnesses accumulate and form a revolution that leads to a kinder world—a world in which we care for each other's hearts and our own, so our nerves are calm, allowing us to use our fight or flight energy in more productive ways for each other, our work culture, and the world. A world where every-one—regardless of class or race or socio-economic back-ground—realizes that kindness is a superpower we carry in our hearts, a superpower we can engage at any moment, and one that, when we consistently choose it, changes everything. Even better, it is renewable by being kind to yourself first!

To implement and harness this superpower, create the future we want to live in, and build positive connections with others at work, we need to first redefine the expression *in kind*. Traditionally, paying someone *in kind* means giving back what they gave you. Translated, it is like trading necessities, like clothing for food, thus making a fair trade. We often hear it

when someone pays another's unkindness with more unkindness, as in, "Steve punched John in the mouth, and John paid
him back *in kind*."

Because I think it will lead to a happier work world for
everyone, I am on a mission to change that definition and I
need your help. Everyone deserves a work environment like
the one described at the beginning of the chapter. To make that
a reality, we must redefine the concept of paying others (or responding to others) ***in kind.*** Instead of paying others back with
whatever they gave us, what if *in kind* meant **the kindest actions we can envision in any given moment,** no matter the
circumstances or our perception of them?

What if you practiced this repeatedly until the improved
definition becomes a way of being, creating more profound
satisfaction and greater success for everyone? When you use
kindness as your compass, if a workmate yells, uses sarcasm,
or badmouths you, you can remind them of your shared goals,
the beautiful results that come when you work together, and
how your current disagreement is a temporary obstacle that
you are sure you can overcome together. Try to see the hurt
person hidden behind the bad behavior and remind yourself
that they are trying to hurt you only because of how hard
things feel for them, not because of the argument at hand. Also, you don't have to control, or take responsibility for, anyone's words or actions but your own. Kindness is your
superpower, after all.

This kindness practice is like channeling a kung fu master

who dodges or blocks every blow with minimal effort while saying, "Let's be friends. There's no need to fight." An expert in kindness will expend little energy while a verbal or emotional attacker exhausts themselves, gaining nothing.

This book is about understanding and navigating the emotional interplay, politics, friendships, and other layers of your workplace, regardless of whether it is healthy, confusing, disjoint, or downright toxic. It is about obtaining the tools and knowledge needed to handle work situations and feel good about yourself before, during, and after.

These techniques will maximize your chances of seeing significant, positive changes. Best of all, you can stay true to treating your neighbors the way you want to be treated.

Ready to start?

First, let me tell you about a time, before I had my bearings, when I got many things wrong about kindness in the workplace. Let me tell you about Terry.

Soon after I graduated from college, Terry hired me to oversee several core workstreams at a mid-sized niche company. My extensive experience and evident success during a part-time college job landed me a job at a larger and more prestigious company. Terry said it made me "the perfect new leader to handle this group." However, from my first day at the company, coworkers warned me about Terry. "He pretends he understands what's going on, but you probably know ten times more than he does. And you're just a kid out of college."

Two department heads told me not to trust anyone close to

Terry because they reported back the slightest voice of dissent. One of them also mentioned the rage and fury between Terry and my predecessor. "Toward the end, they had a big yelling match. Terry yelled something about Alan trying to take over everything. Alan yelled back, 'At least if I did, we wouldn't have an idiot running the show!' Alan turned in his resignation an hour later."

As if those warning signs weren't enough, one of my new team members asked me never to let Terry talk to her alone. "I can't stand how he scolds me. Ever since my lung transplant, I can't help but move slowly. If I use my scooter, he complains it is a hazard." I wish I could say I'm exaggerating or making up some of these details for dramatic effect. I know they're hard to believe. I was in disbelief, too, and couldn't imagine that kind of behavior.

I settled into the job, hoping none of my new colleagues' warnings would manifest. Within two months, though, nearly every bad behavior they had warned me about showed up taking me from surprise and disbelief to anger and indignation. Surely the Golden Rule—do to others only what you would have done to you—did not apply to a big jerk like Terry, right?

Thus, my voice joined my colleagues' hushed hallway conversations about Terry. I criticized his priorities at meetings he didn't attend. At the privacy of my desk, I showed off Terry's budget for colleagues to point out his lack of attention to detail. I badmouthed Terry in whatever ways fit the narrative my colleagues and I had created. I played the hero to stand against his role as the villain. I did...until Terry called me to his office.

Terry glowered over his desk at me while he repeated a nasty remark I'd made earlier that day that I thought he knew nothing about. I tried to calm my heart while I weaseled my way through our conversation, deflecting his questions. I admitted minor infractions and fled as soon as I could, knowing I had become the worst version of myself, one small compromise, one white lie, one justification at a time. Instead of solving problems, I was morphing into the same kind of monster that I had pictured Terry to be. I saw no way out but to quit.

But even as I moved on from that job, for years afterward, shame burned in my stomach whenever I interacted with new colleagues. When I saw bad behavior in others, a little voice in my head would surface and ask me, "Are you going to whisper about this one, too?" Once, when I put my three young children to bed, that voice mocked me, "When do you teach the kids how to be weasels?" The thing about shame is that while it eats away at you, making you squirm with each internal retelling of some sordid story, it owns you. Most people are afraid to talk about their shameful secrets. Choosing instead to hide them makes them burn more intensely and makes us act out in everyday situations that shouldn't be a big deal. We all have these.

We need more practice naming our mistakes, discussing them, looking for guidance, and learning from them. It was only when I began confronting the stories perpetuated by my shame, examining them one by one in the light, that I finally took ownership of the narrative of my life. At last, I became the storyteller. I began creating the story of my life in a mode of growth informed by mistakes rather than one where my shame would invariably hijack my actions.

Getting past shame, I returned to my roots: believing in kindness as the only defensible action. It is the only choice with the power to create enduring, authentic positive outcomes.

So why do we hide these painful moments in the dark shadows?

In his book *Ego is the Enemy*, Ryan Holiday calls the ego "an unhealthy belief in our own importance," a belief that shows us a distorted view of the world. Your ego tells you that you are unique and amazing, that you shouldn't have to put up with long lines, bad drivers, or hearing the word "no" when you want something. Oddly, your ego also tells you that you are a fraud, an unworthy imposter and that everyone watches your every move because they want to laugh at you. The two extremes reduce to the same issue: exaggeratedly seeing your importance.

The positive side of having a healthy ego is that it acts as a voice within you, stating that you are worthy of kindness and love. The ego serves as a self-defense mechanism in a universe that won't notice if we are left behind or poorly treated. Without an ego, would you ever challenge yourself to do hard things with the belief that you might be able to do them? When given a smaller portion than others at the dinner table, would you speak up for your wish to have an equal share?

An unchecked ego, however, leads you to make neglectful or even cruel decisions related to other people in favor of your personal needs. Wanting more food in a situation where it is scarce is understandable; however, an overblown ego would push you to demand a larger share of food when your ailing grandfather might have a more profound, more pressing need.

When stranded at an airport after missing a flight, who wouldn't want to get the next available flight? The typical traveler asks for help catching that flight; however, a traveler with a runaway ego will throw angry verbal jabs at the airline employee attempting to help. In these ego-driven moments, the grumpy traveler might feel righteously indignant, but to the other stranded travelers, it comes across as abusive and arrogant.

Now, to imagine what you might look like from the outside, let us consider a much larger backdrop—the Universe itself. Whether we behave kindly or shake our fists about the inconveniences we must endure, we engage in those activities on a planet roughly 8,000 miles in diameter. If you were looking at a 12-inch desktop Earth globe, a scale model of you would be $1/600,000^{th}$ of an inch tall. If someone decided to dust that globe, the speck that represents you would be swept away as something on the smallish side of most dust particles, some of which, on this scale, would be the size of six-story buildings. How much would that globe feel the stamping feet of a speck of dust?

Let's go even bigger and less hypothetical. Astronomers have straightforward ways of measuring the distances to faraway objects, from planets in our own Solar System to the most distant galaxies in the visible Universe. Those measurements tell us that our tiny human bodies are roughly 0.00000000000000000000002% the diameter of the known universe. Setting the numbers aside, it is sufficient to understand one simple fact: We are imperceptible and thoroughly inconsequential in the grand scheme of the Universe.

To experience cosmic perspective another way, we can do the same exercise regarding our lifetimes compared to the entire history of the Universe. Using a lengthy lifespan for humans of 100 years and the calculated age of the Universe as 13,800,000,000 years, our lives amount to 0.0000007% of the age of everything that has come before. In other words, we are nothing but a cosmic blink.

Why bring up these facts in the context of our egos? Frankly, because you need to know this vast universe doesn't care about you.

You are a speck, a blink, among billions of specks and blinks on this planet alone. To say that you are incomprehensibly minute on a cosmic scale is an accurate summary. We are all born, we will all die, and in between, we remain laughably small.

That said, there's a flip side that's more important than our size or our longevity: In the sheer enormity of space and time, you are the only *you* that there ever was or ever will be. This means that you are also infinitely unique, precious, and irreplaceable. Even an identical twin whose DNA matches yours will have different experiences. Your preferences, your abilities, and your fates are equally divergent.

No one can replace you.

Considering this, are our egos correct? Are you special? Does it matter if you misbehave?

Your ego is flat-out wrong about your importance in the ways already demonstrated. The Universe hardly notices what you do. Yet, in all the Cosmos, you are unique and special. This contradiction can fill you with awe, wonder, confusion, and annoyance. Still, the universal perspective has something more profound and essential to teach us. It is probably the most powerful and exciting lesson: If *you* are infinitely precious as a unique entity in the cosmos, so are all other humans who have ever lived.

Anyone you have ever met—and the vast billions whom you have no chance of ever knowing during such a short lifetime—every single one is as unique and infinitely precious as you.

Succinctly put, other people are wonders.

They are mysterious and compelling with the potential to enrich our lives when we get the chance to meet and know them. Every person you will ever meet is a marvel.

So, we can choose to act like jerks but arguing and fighting feels like a waste. When we know our time is so short, in the grand scheme of the Universe, whatever it is that might be bugging you takes on far less significance. What justification could we possibly have for treating other people, marvelous wonders that they are, in unkind ways?

Once the worth of others truly sinks in, it seems fitting to consider issues of kind and fair treatment for everyone. With a right-sized ego, consider fairness through a brilliant thought experiment by philosopher John Rawls.

Imagine that you are about to enter a world of your design, where you can decide how much power and money you have, which class and race you are born into, and what sex you are at birth. Until you enter this world, however, you are in an *original position* meaning that you do not have any fore-knowledge of your strength, intelligence, race, class, or role within your designed society. Until you step into this world of your own making, you are behind a *veil of ignorance* that ob-scures your entry point into your personally designed society.

What sort of society would you start with? If you design a community where nearly everyone is a peasant and only a few lucky people are royalty, the veil of ignorance keeps you from knowing if you will be the emperor or just another servant un-til you are there.

Suppose, instead, you design a society where healthcare, food, shelter, and education are guaranteed rights for every-one. In that case, your role in that society will be far less worri-some because you know you will have good odds of having a healthy and supported life.

What sort of society do you hope for? What is the future of your dreams?

Harnessing the best of our hopes and dreams helps to create the vision of the future we desire. Once that vision makes sense, planning and doing the work of building leads to the future we want to live in. Your actions help make that future more or less likely. This responsibility rests on everyone.

When I met Terry's force with my force, the shrapnel blew outward toward everyone, worsening the toxic work culture. Although my lousy behavior with Terry could not single-handedly destroy our chances of a brighter future, the ripple effects of our unkind battles sowed distrust, contributed to stress, and brought us a step further away from that beautiful future I want us all to live in.

I am betting that paying Terry *in kind*—with kindness, support, and curiosity—would have had better results for everyone. Plus, it would have left me feeling more pride and less shame about my choices.

Do you have a coworker who tries to bully you? Is there someone in your life whose personality doesn't mesh with yours?

When you envision yourself equipped with a deep kindness practice, politely and kindly standing your ground with this work bully, you can almost feel the metaphorical fists whooshing past you, right? Even if you take a few punches to the chin, you are strong. At least you saw them coming and had the tools to deflect most of the attacks and keep your composure. You have weathered hard things before and emerged stronger for it.

In the meantime, others will respect you more for standing your ground and giving back kindness. Even the person flailing out at you, for reasons I will discuss later in the book, will start to realize how bad they look in that situation. You might even win them over. Even if they refuse to change, there are ways of being kind to yourself and exiting the situation before more damage occurs.

Adopting this new mode of being within the workplace can feel unnatural, even scary, at first. Exercising a newly realized superpower is like that. However, I can assure you that it is far messier and more painful to remain quiet in a dysfunctional workplace or encounter unkindness in a thoroughly toxic one without adopting the tools I present throughout this book. Lingering in harm's way without a plan is a lonelier process, and very likely will lengthen the duration of potential suffering.

Remember that vision of a fantastic workplace we talked about at the beginning of this chapter? We cannot get there by fighting fire with fire. That future we imagine is only possible when we pay others in kind. The beautiful thing is that the more you pay others in kind, the more others around you will take up your cause, shifting to kinder behaviors, too. Before long, the whole culture turns for the better. The best part is that you didn't have to mount a massive campaign; all you had to do was stand firm, insisting that *you* were kind at every turn.

To start you on this journey, I have created exercises you can use to apply the teachings in this chapter to your situation. These easy, thought-provoking activities will help you develop concrete ideas about changes you can make that will benefit you, everyone around you, and the future of workplace culture.

Before you engage in these exercises, a last couple of words about the journey you are embarking on. Kindness is your superpower. You can use it whenever you have sufficient energy and a little courage. We will talk in later chapters about self-care (i.e., kindness to yourself) and how it helps you recharge your batteries enough to be kind to others.

As for courage, it will have to come from a place of genuine belief, and that's where we can start right now.

CHAPTER 1 EXERCISES

Exercise 1: Your Beliefs About Kindness

Write your beliefs about the following three concepts in a dedicated journal, notebook, or digital application like One-Note. Write a few sentences or bullet points about what each thought or phrase means to you:

1. The Golden Rule: Do unto others as you would have done to you.

2. The Silver Rule: Do not do to others what you would not have done to you.

3. Kind treatment of others AND yourself.

Even if your responses to the above change over time, writing your beliefs helps clarify what you feel is essential. When difficult situations test how well you uphold your beliefs, you can revisit them and develop better strategies (see below).

Exercise 2: Your Ideal Workplace

In your journal, describe what your ideal workplace is like. Don't hold back on descriptions. Focus more on the human interactions. How does everyone know what behaviors are expected and acceptable? When someone behaves in unacceptable ways, who handles it and how? When things get busy or complicated, how do people help each other?

Exercise 3: Fighting Fire with Fire

On a new page of your journal, write about experiences where you had troubling or difficult interactions with a colleague. If you have yet to engage in difficult interactions, rely on real-world interactions you have witnessed or heard about directly.

1. Write down any instance where you met someone else's force with force. Leave space below each instance for notes.

2. List repercussions for each interaction you listed, big or small. (Did you "win?" How were your relationships after that? Were there lingering downsides, such as fear of retaliation, lost trust, or broken relationships?)

3. Write down three ways you could use more kindness in similar situations in the future.

4. Next, in your journal, note:

- situations in which you were less kind than you wish you had been.

- alternative strategies that might have helped you align with your beliefs about kindness.

5. Write down any situations where not acting nor speaking up is resulting in unkind consequences for you or others.

- Briefly describe the situation.

- Are there factors that are holding you back? What are they? What are you doing to try to create a more positive flow?

- Are there ways you could speak up or act now or in the future when a similar situation arises? What are they?

- Who are allies you can enlist in future situations? Will you communicate your needs to them in private? When will you enlist them: ahead of time, during, or after the uncomfortable situation has occurred?

Exercise 4: Your Ego

1. Write up to three instances *in life* when your ego took over.

   - Examples: Yelling at a customer service agent. Chasing down a driver who cut you off on the highway.

2. Write down any instances *at work* when your ego took over.

   - Examples: Talking over others during a meeting because you were sure you knew more about the topic. Gossiping about a colleague who got something you thought you deserved, like a better raise, better project, or a promotion.

3. Write down the kindest assumptions about the others involved in those situations.

   - Examples: They cut me off in traffic because they were on their way to the hospital to see a dying relative for the last time. My colleague got that cool project because they had relevant experience in college that I didn't know about.

NOTES ABOUT THESE EXERCISES

- By being concrete about situations that challenge the firmness of your beliefs, you are taking control of your behavior and building a strategy to help you be the person you wish to be.

- If you envision it, you can create it. It is impossible to hit a target you can't see.

- By thinking about others' motivations, you can remember that challenging situations frequently have nothing to do with you.

- Building better relationships and creating positive connections with others at work begins with reflection. The more mindful you are in these exercises, the more you will understand relationships at work.

CHAPTER 2
SURPASS YOUR LIMITS

Now that you have set down your beliefs on kindness, learned how and why we should treasure the people around us, and have heightened motivation to be deliberate about being kind, there are hidden undercurrents in the workplace that we need to discuss. To be efficient in using our kindness means we must anticipate how others may receive it. We must understand our colleagues and our own personal hidden world, where limiting beliefs are rampant but remain unspoken or poorly understood. We must also understand the limitations put on us by societal expectations and systems that may not be obvious.

When you show up to a new job, you are surrounded by coworkers you know nothing about. Getting to know them takes time. Even after you think you see a colleague well, some of their behaviors can still be a mystery. Multiply this issue times the number of people you work with, and it can seem daunting. Putting yourself in their shoes, it is easy to imagine them having a similar challenge when learning about you.

It turns out that we may not even know *ourselves* all that well. To understand ourselves, we have to go on a journey of self-awareness. When we reflect on our motivations, actions, and moments of shame, we can come up with treasures. They need cleaning and polishing, but they will ultimately change everything about how you exist in the workplace and at home.

Reflect on a situation in your life when you felt intense emotions, especially if that situation is one that you have seen someone else handle easily. Perhaps you were at your wits end and got snappy with someone. Maybe you felt deep embarrassment or the urge to run, hide, or cry. What the heck is going on inside you, or any of us, in moments like these?

A lot of what you learned about safety, kindness, love, gratitude, anger, fear, and the world around you came from your experiences of being a baby and then a toddler, even though you may not be able to recall those times. Whether or not your conscious mind can remember it is irrelevant. The fact is that you experienced the world during those years. Those experiences shaped you on a nonverbal and unconscious level. From your babyhood through this moment, you have steadily grown into the person you are now.

What about the rest of childhood that you *can* recall? Many of us don't try to think back to our experiences from age seven, but we carry those experiences with us, too. If we did contemplate what we remember from those years, it could hold a

treasure trove of what we believe and want for our lives. Regardless, those experiences shape our relationships with those
around us, whether we know it or not.

Now imagine a meeting with your coworkers. What kinds
of undercurrents exist? Will you spot them? Not noticing or
understanding unstated emotions is Kryptonite to your superpower, kindness. Kind acts can backfire, destabilize a situation, and leave you perplexed and tired.

When a sensitive topic arises and affects you in hidden
ways you don't fully understand, you could act misaligned
with your beliefs, values, and long-term goals. If the topic triggers a key stakeholder in that meeting, prompting them to act
negatively, then what? The shape of your next project, or possibly the next step in your career, could hang in the balance, so
let's get you ready for these moments.

Focusing on experiences from your youth is in order.
Knowing more about these experiences is essential to understanding how you show up in your personal and work life.
Once you have detailed insights about what sticks in your
memory, you can use those insights to make your work life
better.

Let me share an example from my life to illustrate the
point.

When I was old enough to understand getting grades from
school, my parents let my sister, Brenda, and me know they
wanted our report cards filled with good ones. Dad lectured us
many times about a good life being available only to those

who studied hard and proved they were intelligent and capable. How? You guessed it–through good grades.

However, one perplexing element of this situation was this: it was acceptable for me to get worse grades than my older sister. Brenda needed top marks in all classes to escape parental lectures, but I could earn lower scores and avoid extensive finger-wagging.

When I was ten, we went on a family vacation at the end of a school term. I was sitting comfortably on the couch at a beach house when my father announced that he would like to see our grades. While my sister was grilled about a single sub-par "B," I dreaded parental reactions to my report card filled primarily with sub-par grades. Their reactions? A passing comment from Dad: "Please give it some more effort." A reassurance from Mom: "We know you are doing your best." That was it.

My sister's understandable reaction was to be angry at the little brother who seemed to get away with mediocrity. This is the interesting thing about individual experiences: I absorbed a completely different message than you might expect. Rather than relishing my parents' lower expectations, I wondered why my family did not care about me as much as they did my sister.

I mean, they spent more time encouraging her, pushing her, and lecturing her. Why not do the same with me? Perhaps, my ten-year-old mind pondered, I was not worthy of those attentions. So began my life-long limiting belief: *nobody cares about me.*

Who knows why my parents held my sister to a higher standard? Perhaps, as a boy, my parents assumed I would automatically have an easier life; thus, my scholastic efforts did not need much scrutiny. The grades were good, if not stellar, so why push? They might have thought they needed to worry about my sister to ensure she would have a good life. Or, perhaps, her higher IQ score made them more focused on her. Or, maybe, they had pushed their firstborn more, as many parents do. Yet, when my child-mind claimed the story, *nobody cares about me*, does it matter what motivations my parents had?

Years later, when my sister and I discussed this and her "you got away with things" narrative collided with my "nobody cares about me" narrative, we realized we had two completely different perceptions of reality. This sort of thing can happen in any relationship.

It is worth noting that I recognize that my parents love me and that I know how privileged I am. So, why do I have an overriding, pervasive sense that nobody cares about me? How can (at least) two conflicting perspectives simultaneously feel viscerally true to me?

The short answer is that emotions do not care about logic.

The slightly longer answer is that emotional processes within the human brain do not always align with logical ones. While you can feel several conflicting emotions at the same time, the rational mind tries to make sense of the world in yes-no, on-off terms. It ponders solutions, makes plans, and pays attention to the passage of time. Emotions feel unrestrained by time, so when you are in a particularly intense emotional state, you say or think, "This will never end." When making decisions about your life, every one of your brain processes gets a vote.

The amygdala, the hippocampus, and other portions of the human brain enable us to feel, process, and connect our emotions to memories. These centers of our brain shape our decision-making processes. In real-world terms, this means we might believe we make logical decisions aligned with our goals based on our declared values while, in fact, we make decisions based primarily on our emotions and instincts.

In my deep-seated belief that others didn't care about me, I unconsciously fed that narrative, like when I missed the fourth-grade student government yearbook photos. I thought I heard the announcement over the school loudspeaker for our group to report for picture-taking. When I convinced myself I had heard it correctly, nine-year-old me stepped into the hallway only to see the picture being taken at the other end of the hall...without me.

I wondered if they were happier that I wasn't in the picture. I even went so far as to think, "Maybe I was kicked out, and nobody told me?"

We all latch onto beliefs in our younger years based more on emotion than on logic. These can quietly guide our thought processes and decisions in everyday life without our explicit consent. We call these beliefs based exclusively on emotion, often in the face of contrary facts, *limiting beliefs.* They drive us to act in ways that don't acknowledge reality and might even counter our best interests or those around us. Commonly, we don't even know we have these limiting beliefs or that they influence us unless we tease them out and carefully think about them. These beliefs can seem perfectly logical, or they might be firmly emotional and lacking in logic, like a janitor's child believing it is impossible to become a college professor, or the daughter of a perpetually-abused wife who never left her husband finding herself unable to end her own rocky marriage, even though she says she wants to; or the son of a dentist who believes candy is so evil that he develops eating disorders.

What are your limiting beliefs?

When you dig into the exercises at the end of this chapter, you will prepare yourself to listen for subtext at work. Some of this relates to understanding yourself well enough to know what topics stimulate your emotions. Perhaps even more powerful than understanding your own responses to various situations is the fact that knowing about limiting beliefs helps you understand outsized emotional reactions from colleagues, bosses, corporate leaders, customers, supporters, and anyone else you encounter at work.

The more you understand what motivates you and others, the more you can navigate situations and bring out kindness as a healing element. If a conversation gets heated, you can ask to pause and come back to said discussion later. Suppose you can tell by a person's body language, facial expressions, or words that they are having an outsized reaction to a particular topic. In this case, you can make reasonable guesses about why they have had that big emotion—they have some limiting beliefs that need to be explored. Choosing to get curious about that reaction, instead of defensive or angry, gives you something tangible to work with instead of just swimming around in strong emotions yourself. You have a potent tool, knowing to ask questions at all.

What about self-care? Kindness toward yourself allows you to recharge your superpower. The most obvious example is that studies show we make kinder decisions after a satisfying sleep or a good meal. If the reverse is true and you had horrible sleep or are "hangry," your ability to kindly support and care for others dramatically diminishes.

The more you feel good about your health and general circumstances, the more you replenish the renewable resource of kindness. If you are engaging in regular self-care, you decrease obstacles related to your kindness practice. Therefore, a simple trick for removing or reducing limitations on your kindness superpower is to care for yourself consistently and authentically.

What's more, knowing about your limiting beliefs helps you do two things at work better than before. First, you can consider how you might be showing up in various circumstances that could make you act in ways you don't want to and plan accordingly. Second, it helps you remember that every colleague you encounter, either during meetings or in the hallway, also has limiting beliefs. Knowing more about why outsized emotional reactions happen to us all will enable you to put a strategy around the ones you're dealing with either in yourself or others.

A bonus activity you can add to the exercise below is listing key colleagues' potential limiting beliefs. Consider a colleague who appears to have knee-jerk reactions or significant emotional reactions to a common situation. Every time you bring up the idea of spending part of an established budget, your supervisor immediately says no. Instead of automatically concluding that the supervisor is unreasonable, doesn't see the bigger picture, or does not like your ideas, perhaps something deeper is going on. Maybe your supervisor's "no!" reflects a limiting belief from their childhood when the family finances were tight, and reserves needed to be preserved.

Any of these suppositions may not be accurate. Still, your guesses might be close enough that you can start informal conversations (away from budget topics) that lead to more answers. This detective work can pay huge dividends as you learn more about your colleagues. Even with little information, you can remind yourself that others show up with their limiting beliefs, which can cause them to act unexpectedly. This new approach can transform your relationships at work, allowing you to employ your kindness practice consistently. Even more amazing, you can craft your responses to the people and the situation in front of you more accurately and authentically.

Thinking about your side of the equation, you will benefit greatly by knowing your limiting beliefs. It will help you stay alert to your conscious and unconscious motivations, reminding you to consider the big picture. The result is that you will possess two sets of strategies—one for showing up as your best self, and the other for taking care of others.

What about limits that are not internal but exist in the framework of our society? Regardless of what country you grew up in or live in, societies treat different groups of people differently. How can you recognize limits put on you and on others? How can you help those who face the most significant challenges? How can you improve your odds of overcoming these limits?

Philosopher John Rawls laid out an idealized way of designing a society that values equity by having designers behind a veil of ignorance while making their designs. Still, only some societies come close to that ideal. The United States of America has a much-heralded free society ideal, but talk to people of color, women, children, people who practice religion outside the few considered mainstream, or anyone in the LGBTQIA+ community, and they'll tell you otherwise. Other countries on Earth, past and present, have had challenges regarding society members feeling valued, so the USA is hardly unique in this struggle. So, what can we do about it?

To help yourself, it is best to understand your status within society. This can be calculated in the fourth exercise below. Still, in general terms, you can add (or subtract) from your overall score for each factor you see society as valuing or devaluing you. Use the information you discover to understand the importance of joining (or starting) groups that champion those with less privilege or lower societal standing and then work with those groups. One clear example is women in the United States before 1920. They did not have the right to vote. When those women joined together to protest society's unjust treatment, they did so at significant cost and with great effort. They recruited allies in the form of progressive men who understood what great benefits society would gain by hearing diverse voices in the voting bloc. By engaging people with more social standing, they enhanced the culture and changed their status within that society. This resulted in the 19th Amendment to the U.S. Constitution preventing discrimination in voting on the basis of sex.

Plenty of other examples appear in countries' histories around the world as those with lower status banded together to gain better treatment within their societies. Understanding history and understanding your perceived value within your society are two factors that can help you determine actions that can help you gain better standing. In the everyday working world, it could be as simple as connecting with others of like mind, similar social positions, and allies so that you can voice concerns.

It can be heartening and beneficial to work at companies that align with and support those who understand the limits placed on them societally. Some companies dub these groups Employee Resource Groups (ERGs). Wherever they exist, you will find women, members of the LGBTQIA+ community, people of Asian descent, Black and African-Americans, Latino/Latinx and Hispanics, veterans, and people with disabilities and their allies giving voices to their concerns. For those with more power, wealth, and privilege, helping others—being an ally to these groups—is an honor and a worthwhile pursuit. After all, if every human we meet is a marvelous wonder, how could we do otherwise? The best advice I have heard on being a great ally includes listening, self-education through books and movies, and getting training in how to be a good ally. As you interact with others, try to avoid assuming anything about their needs or worries and instead employ listening, believing, and supporting in ways that are asked of you. From one country to the next, these groups could be very different in composition and not always in ways predictable by the casual observer, so again, self-education is vital to understanding.

Take your time with the following exercises. The first four can make you seem like a mind-reader the more you practice and deepen your answers. The last exercise can help you better understand the spectrum of limits that others would impose on us and how to proceed to overcome those.

Do you want to go deeper? Check out my free resources on www.michaelgneece.com to start planning how to overcome what could be holding you back.

CHAPTER 2 EXERCISES

Exercise 1: Discovering Your Limiting Beliefs and Taking Action

Take this survey of common limiting beliefs to determine which ones might be relevant to you. Review the common limiting beliefs below and determine if any evoke a strong emotional, visceral response. As you do this, you might think of limiting beliefs that are not listed that apply to you, so write those down too. Record them in your journal.

I need to know what to do.	It is my job to make you happy.	People are judging me.
No one cares about me.	I need a partner to be happy.	People should be self-sufficient.
I know what's best.	It is my fault.	They should agree with me.
I deserve bad treatment.	I should be different.	I have to work hard.
Something terrible is going to happen.	I missed my chance.	We must keep our promises.
Most people cannot be trusted.	Never settle.	I have to be careful not to hurt others.
People should respect me.	People should listen to me.	Money will make me happy.

I need to control how others feel about me.	I'm not enough.	I'm ashamed of my body.
I feel your energy.	I am a failure.	I need to be in control.
I need more money.	I will never make you happy.	My body should be healthy.
Life isn't fair.	I need to understand.	People need to be more trustworthy.
The world should be filled with love.	I need to do it right.	Take what you can when you can.
Some people will never listen.	Nobody can control me.	There is a purpose to my life.
I cannot stay undecided.	Something is wrong with me.	I am worthless.
I can't do anything right.	Be happy with what you have.	Life is difficult.
I disappoint people.	S/he doesn't trust me.	People should be grateful.
I don't want to look foolish.	The world is not safe.	I am a fraud.
There's too much to do.	I shouldn't be so emotional.	I don't belong.
There's not enough time.	Nothing is reliable.	Rule breakers should be punished.
I know what you need.	I must know my life's purpose.	People are my friends.

In your journal, center on the strongest belief first. Which statement jumped out at you? If you thought of a new one while scanning the others, what was it? Was it the strongest? Once you have decided which statement is most potent, focus on it. Later, you can move to the second-most powerful message and do the following for it, and so forth.

Ponder how it could have originated. Was it the interactions within your family unit? Was it at school? Having a reasonable idea of where you picked up your belief can help you center on it and address it head-on.

Once you have some ideas written in your journal about the origins of the belief, the next step is to envision that belief as if it were a living, breathing entity that, at one time or another, served to protect you. Forgive it for the heartache and difficulties it may be causing now that you no longer need it. Thank it for the upsides as well, like realizing that the belief that you need to hoard money led you to more fiscal responsibility in household finances.

My belief can make me feel excluded when projects are assigned, and I have no role, although I know I could contribute. My supervisor can push me off and, noting that he has plenty of time for my peers, I can worry that I have lost value in his eyes.

Knowing I have this limiting belief gives me power since I can spot these emotional reactions and put them into context. I may have no role on a project because a bigger project will need my attention soon. Maybe my supervisor knows that my peers need extra support right now, and didn't he give me his full, undivided attention just last week?

List your negative responses to situations and how they relate to your limiting belief. Come up with at least one strategy for reframing the problem so that you can calm your emotions when they come up again.

In this next part, you will own the narrative: write down each belief's positives in your life.

Taking my "nobody cares about me" belief as an example, what could the positives be for such a belief? It can be easy to dwell only on the negative sides of my limiting belief. Still, there are upsides to these beliefs, and the upside is always your powerful ability to adapt to life because of the challenges you had to overcome.

The upside to my limiting belief is that I persistently seek ways to ensure others around me feel noticed, heard, lifted, and cared for. In every job I have held since the age of 19, I have made it a point to ensure colleagues and friends know how to get support. I have written guidebooks on how to be good at various roles at each workplace so that others would always feel safe. Before new colleagues join, I brainstorm how to make them feel genuinely welcomed, setting out gifts and giving them helpful tips in a welcome email. I put recurring notices on digital calendars regarding work anniversaries and reach out to celebrate those dates. I join social clubs and community organizations where I can volunteer my time to make the workplace happier and more fulfilling. I have even gone so far as to create community organizations at work where none existed to give others a sense of belonging and better support than they might otherwise have felt.

What are the upsides of your beliefs? List them in your journal entry and expand on any that need more explanation.

Repeat the process for any other beliefs you feel deeply.

Exercise 2: Establish Strategies for Showing Up as Your Best Self

In your journal, list every way you know of to put yourself into the best headspace to utilize the positives of your limiting beliefs. Most of these can feel obvious after you have written them down, but it is invaluable to do so.

Consider these items for your list: eating a healthy breakfast daily; exercising regularly; staying hydrated; listing at least three things you are grateful for at the start of each day.

After that general list, make a list of strategies for handling difficult moments in the workday. Those might include assuming positive intent on the part of someone who seems at odds with you over a particular topic or in a particular moment; getting curious and asking questions rather than declaring your frustration and anger as a knee-jerk response; and reminding colleagues of your successful past collaborations and of your mutual commitment to project or company goals.

Review these strategies before any workday that you think could be tricky. Review these strategies after a workday presenting severe challenges.

Exercise 3: Create Strategies for Moments When You're Not at Your Best

Make a list of your triggers. You know, the types of challenges that put you at risk for acting and reacting in ways you want to avoid. Having this list can save you headaches because you will more easily spot those moments and actions, access more compassion for yourself, and choose to be kind instead of reacting.

Consider these items for your list: someone cutting you off when you are speaking; someone not making eye contact with you or someone else at the table; and anything related directly to your limiting belief, such as budget discussions if your limiting belief has created money worries.

For those items related to your limiting beliefs, list ways you think you can stay open-minded and optimistic. Consider letting others know that you sometimes feel outsized reactions to a particular topic before the discussions occur so that they understand any lapses in your positivity around that topic. By humanizing yourself, you help them know you better while simultaneously role-modeling how to better relate to others, and you become a better version of yourself.

Exercise 4: Create Strategies for Caring for Others

When others do not show up as their best selves at work, how can you make them feel valued, supported, and at ease? Depending on the situation and your knowledge of the colleague in question, this can be tricky. Seeing a colleague crying at their desk can feel clear-cut, knowing that it is kind to check in with them and ask if they need someone to talk to or sit with. What about another scenario where your supervisor is grouchy?

My favorite suggestion is to get curious and ask questions. Sometimes humor can masquerade as curiosity, so you should only use humor if you know with great confidence how it will land with your audience. Humor, especially sarcasm, can be deeply triggering and garner poor outcomes. Asking how your colleague or supervisor feels or if they are okay shows unambiguously that you care and want to be helpful.

In your journal, list ways to show colleagues that you care, that you can be trusted, and that are likely to dissipate tension in difficult situations. Part of that list could include mentally reviewing what you know about the colleague's recent life events, such as difficult medical news, problems at home with a spouse, child, or parent, or if they had car troubles recently. You can even note what brings joy and comfort to specific colleagues.

Exercise 5: Understanding the External Limits on You

The following exercise will help you get a rough estimate of your perceived social status within the United States of America. Start with a score of 10 and add/subtract points as directed.

1. Wealth: If you are wealthy, add a point. If you are middle class, make no changes. If you live in poverty, subtract a point.

2. Gender: If you are male, add a point. If female, make no changes. If you are part of the gender spectrum outside of male and female (i.e. non-binary, asexual, etc.), subtract a point.

3. Race: If you are white, add a point; otherwise, subtract a point.

4. Sexual Orientation: If you are heterosexual, add a point.

5. Ethnicity: Add a point if you are non-Hispanic/non-Latino.

6. Origin: If you were born in the US, add a point. If you were born in any other country, make no changes.

7. Religion: If you are Christian, add a point. If you are any other religion, make no changes. If you are atheist or agnostic, subtract a point.

8. Political Party: If you are Democrat or Republican, add a point EXCEPT whenever interacting with the "opposite" of what you chose, in which case subtract a point. If you are neither Democrat nor Republican, subtract a point.

9. Disability: If you are non-disabled, add a point. If you are disabled, subtract a point.

10. Age: Add a point if you are between 16 and 65. If not, make no changes.

It is crucial to understand that your score reflects your societal status and is not a measure of your worth. Regardless of any score, you are a marvelous wonder, so bear that in mind.

Whenever you have added and subtracted all the points as advised above to arrive at a final score, write down your score here: _____. If your score is 20, your perceived status in the United States is at its peak. The farther your score is below 20, the more externally imposed limits you face.

The vast majority of people in America have some level of privilege and some limits when measured this way. The good news is that you likely have groups you can be an ally to. The other good news is that more groups are probably trying to support you than you can name or count if you have any of the societal limits measured in this score.

An Important Note: As we improve society, we raise scores. As we build the future we want to live in, one kind act at a time, we support those who are perceived as "lesser" and, thereby, shift the hearts and minds of more and more people. A genuinely equitable society won't be able to perceptibly quantify differences in societal status using a scoring system like the one above because trying to do so won't even make sense. All the scores would be between 9.5 and 10.5, and adding or subtracting whole points based on any factors would be unimaginable. We can get there together. Meanwhile, find groups who support you as you face limits put upon you and join other groups to help those who need you as an ally in their fight.

In other countries, many factors could be the same, but adding or subtracting a single point might be too little or too much, so partner with someone you trust and develop your own system of factors and points. Ultimately, the exact point amounts and the factors we use can be debated. What is certain, however, is that in nearly any community on Earth at this moment, there are measurable differences in how different types of people are viewed and treated. It is neither fair nor is it healthy. To build the world we want to live in, we need to reduce the points counted and the factors that matter as close to zero as possible.

The good news is that we can change the world the more we think about these systems and work with others to improve them. What is the best and kindest way forward?

CHAPTER 3
WHO AM I?

O nce we examine our limits, even if we cannot remove them altogether, the next thing to understand and conquer is the age-old question: "Who am I?"

Many of us start jobs long before we think deeply about how the shapes of our careers will affect so much of our lives. Perhaps, we factor in two or three generic factors, such as how much a profession can help us earn, how to showcase what we're already good at, or how pleased our friends and family members will be. How often do we reach for a new job thinking about how it aligns with who we are or hope to become?

Generally, after listening to our friends, family, and college professors' advice, we apply for available positions and take what looks like a good offer. Before we know it, we could be a few years down a path that feels more like a trap than a career.

I felt lost and empty when I was a few jobs into my working life. It wasn't that the jobs were bad ones, but it always felt like I had stumbled into a workplace where other people knew why they were there while I did not. It felt like a big secret that I had no clue why I was there. The longer I stayed, the more I picked up skills and knowledge everyone valued, so the more I was promoted and given meaningful projects. Meaningful to someone, but often not to me.

By the time you have worked for a few years, you, too, might feel sleepless, anxious, worried, and even lost. It might finally hit you: Enough of this! I am meant for something else! I don't even know why I'm in this job! Isn't there more to life than what I'm doing right now?

Many of us dread the question, "What do you want?" because we have been conditioned to think that a reprimand is coming when we answer. For example, if you think of saying out loud that you want more pay at work, more sex in your romantic relationship, a nicer home, or a kinder boss, do you worry about who will overhear you? You may feel trepidation over even saying one or several of those things aloud with crystal clarity. But...

It is okay to want the things you genuinely want.

Pretend that poetry is a driving force in your life. It is discouraging if you constantly wish for a life dedicated to poetry but hear authority figures telling you that there is no money in that. If you deny your passion for poetry, you will cut off a deep-seated desire, increasing your chances of greater unhappiness. Desires are not just okay to have; they are crucial to mental health. Self-care is vital to keeping your kindness practice strong, consistent, authentic, and dedicated. Denying a motivating force will make self-care difficult as stress emerges in unhealthy behaviors.

Consider this other quandary: If you suppress a substantial portion of who you are, then you are being incredibly unkind to yourself. Stifling the beliefs about what forces drive you makes your values murky and ill-defined. You live daily with the inner conflict of wanting to be true to yourself while working at a job that feels deeply untrue. That internal conflict makes it much easier to look skeptically at others, assuming they are being untrue to themselves. It makes it hard to figure out how to treat others when we have such a hard time figuring out how to be true to ourselves. We risk our ability to show up in kind.

You are the only person responsible for building the life you want. You might feel like your early work life was wasted, but please don't think like that. Instead, consider all the great networking you did and the savvy and know-how you picked up along the way. Remember that you sharpened some skills you probably don't even consider now.

So, what's next?

You can carefully craft a vision of your life and work to make it a reality. Apart from relying on yourself, what other choices do you have? You can let other people, well-intentioned or not, steer your ship. Or, you can do nothing and allow events to happen to you. Just remember that if you don't create a plan of your own, you leave yourself at the mercy of sheer dumb luck or family and friends who don't understand your hopes and dreams as well as you do.

Want help? Go to www.michaelgneece.com to download free tips on how to start outlining your dream job. Let these free pointers guide you so you can make it all work.

Even if you think you already have your life's path clearly in mind, taking time to spell it out can help you gain new clarity and act faster. Since your precious life is the most valuable asset you can control—at least to some extent—isn't it worth your time to be deliberate?

Writing your ideas and selecting relevant images to create a "vision board" is a fruitful exercise. Grab your journal and prepare for a few prompts if you prefer writing only. If you choose a vision board, take photos and phrases symbolizing what you want out of life and put them together digitally or on an actual poster or corkboard. An exercise at the end of this chapter gives more background and a step-by-step procedure for creating a vision board.

Before you try these exercises, test the clarity about your beliefs, values, goals, and life's purpose. Make an audio or video recording of yourself attempting to explain it in under two minutes as if you are explaining it to a stranger. Keep that handy for later.

Next, try the exercise of writing out the vision of your life or creating a vision board. (See the end of the chapter.)

Try the audio/video recording exercise again when you finish these exercises. This time, refer to your vision. If you try two or three times, preserve your favorite version so you can look at it again in the future.

It should come as no surprise if you struggled with the first recording. If it felt more comfortable, or at least more successful, the second time you made the recording, that should prove that taking time to spell out what you want is time well spent.

The danger in not taking this set of exercises seriously is simple: it is hard, if not impossible, to aim for a target that does not exist.

If you skipped over all those steps above and just kept reading, at least jot down a few notes for now, and you can do the activity later. These short prompts can be helpful.

- Who am I?

- What can prompt me to act?

- What things drain my energy and make me unlikely to act?

- What are my goals?

- What do I believe?

We all have forces that compel us to be who we are. Some care deeply about climate change, others about people experiencing homelessness, and others about monster trucks. Still others care about space exploration, food, well-crafted movies, or sports teams. Millions of good answers exist regarding the big question of what drives us. So, please, be honest and try not to judge yourself.

So, what is your purpose? How can you find it?

Envision important, inspiring moments from your life—your childhood, school, meeting a dear friend, or any past jobs—and think and write about those moments. Look for common themes.

A thought process that has helped me refocus my life goals is what I call the Thirteen-Year-Old Me test. Whenever I ponder what I want to do with my life, recalling my thirteen-year-old self's goals and desires centers me on what I find instinctively, powerfully appealing. It is sometimes helpful to have a hypothetical conversation with him that gives me the guidance I need.

Does it seem like your inner thirteen-year-old has more questions than answers? Did that version of you have little control over life? At a guess, just like me, you answered yes to both questions. So, why ask questions of that version of ourselves?

As early teens, we have genuine, unfiltered excitement and curiosity about who we can become. Think of it as an internal compass. Outside forces might try to deflect it from true north, and, over the years, we might allow it to happen in the name of "compromise." Even if you had discouraging adult figures trying to deflect that needle right from the start, there was an instinct that your drives and desires were accurate regardless.

I bet when you listen that 13-year-old voice rings true and is still worth listening to.

For me, I devoured science fiction stories about alien

worlds, travels through time and space, and inventions like spaceships and robots. When I was ten, I read *Tunnel in the Sky* by Robert Heinlein, and in it, I found myself alongside young survivalists trapped in an alien world. Isaac Asimov's short story collection *I, Robot,* drew me into a world of wondering if robots had feelings and if they could harm people. In Ray Bradbury's *Martian Chronicles,* I read—with my jaw dropped— tales of telepathic Martians who tried to kill human invaders from Earth. Some of these stories sent shivers down my spine when I heard them as radio plays made in the 1950s.

As a thirteen-year-old, I devoured science fiction on television as well. The British TV show *Doctor Who* featured multiple actors playing the same role, that of a wise alien Time Lord called The Doctor, a helper of the downtrodden and defender of good and just causes. He traveled anywhere in space and time with companions, always trying to learn and to help, then disappearing to more adventures.

The point in giving you a snapshot of my thirteen-year-old world is simple: The compass I followed at that age still feels like an accurate indicator of what fascinates and inspires me. Reflecting on who I was, who I've always been, clarifies how I should spend at least part of my time as an adult.

Why might your inner compass point more toward movies, gardening, fine cuisine, or international politics, while mine points to science fiction and storytelling?

I bet you have compelling forces that draw you to music, art, friendships, nature walks, books, business, or a hundred other things. I suggest that some early version of you felt these more clearly than you might feel now. When you feel uncertain, a fantastic decision-making method is to ask, "What would thirteen-year-old me want for my life now?"

If the answers feel helpful, consider those answers as you decide your life's path. I find it a valuable exercise even at my stage of life.

Several less introspective methods exist to discover more about yourself and to see how your personality type can be understood and communicated to others. Several standard surveys are used in the professional world to learn more about what motivates you.

The Myers-Briggs Type Indicator personality inventory helps you understand how you see, and others interact with the world around you. It uses four fundamental measurements: introversion versus extroversion; sensing versus intuition; thinking versus feeling; and judging versus perceiving. One finding stands out when I think of my Myers-Briggs profile: introversion versus extroversion.

Knowing that I am an extrovert, meaning that I derive energy from being around people, is beneficial. Perhaps more helpful is that I know my friend Drew, an introvert, recharges by being alone. He and I have different expectations of each other because we know we are different in this way. Understanding this has been crucial to making our friendship strong.

To better understand your colleagues and yourself, ask your supervisor or human resources business partner if personality surveys are available. Usually, you and your teammates take a survey, then a professional reviews the results individually, then as a group.

If your employer does not offer something like this, an alternative is to find a survey online and take it yourself. You can then explore how famous leaders, artists, musicians, and others are categorized by the same survey. This can give better insight into how you see yourself in the world while also giving you insight into the fact that not everyone has the same experiences you have.

Another excellent survey, the DISC Assessment, presents you with a series of questions like the Myers-Briggs; however, the result is for you to find out how much you are driven to see the world in terms of Dominance, Influence, Steadiness, and Conscientiousness. The benefit comes from understanding differences among your colleagues and how you see the world and prefer things. A great example of benefiting from DISC is to know that some people tend to prefer direct communications while others prefer softer, more diplomatic communications.

Author Andres Tapia describes a situation in which he, being from a country and culture that values direct communications, struggled to find positive interactions with several female colleagues from the American South who all preferred diplomacy. "When they told me, 'We agree with you 100%. We would want to tweak these things about what you propose,' what I heard was that we all agreed 100%, and anything on their list after that involved minor tweaks. What I didn't know was that they disagreed with me 100% and didn't want to say that out loud and that the list they gave was actually how they wanted things."

Having lived in the South for most of my life, I can attest to how real this is—stating things diplomatically to the point that the headline is buried after baloney statements of agreement. Not everyone does it, but it is common. It usually appears when the parties involved don't know each other well but must work together toward a common goal.

Regardless of your workplace's use of a personality inventory survey, the results are powerful enough that I strongly recommend you seek out surveys from the list below and take online versions. Most employers will support professional development with funding set aside for you and your colleagues, so seek approval and sign up.

Another powerful way of knowing yourself is understanding how your brain processes information. Perhaps you have heard that we have two wolves inside us—one "good" wolf and one "bad" wolf. Which wolf you choose to feed is the wolf that thrives. An easy example is wishing for an unhealthy sweet treat while also wishing for better health that comes with eating better foods. If you choose to listen to the thought that says, "Eat the unhealthy treat," then you are feeding the "bad" wolf.

While I like the concept in general terms, this feels more complex. Our minds are flooded with input from 40 million pieces of information at any moment, such as background noises and smells, the pressure of your bum against your seat, the lighting conditions around you, and so forth. Your brain "bubbles up" the information you care most about depending on your beliefs, values, to-do lists, and survival factors. By survival factors, I mean that if you hear a fire alarm going off, your subconscious mind had better prioritize that sound and get you to safety.

In short, we do not have just two wolves. We have millions.

Think of all the stray thoughts you have at any moment. The mundane (like how hungry you might be), the more exciting (like anticipating a vacation), and anything in between seem rational and normal. Some thoughts are kind and loving, others are cruel and petty, and others are utterly bizarre or horrifying. The good news is that we are not our thoughts. We choose which thoughts to act on, i.e., which wolves to feed.

A portion of our brain called the Reticular Activation System (RAS) directs thought traffic in your mind, bringing you surface thoughts related to what you deem important. If you learn a new word, you suddenly see it everywhere. If you have decided to travel to a new city, you suddenly notice online articles and overhear conversations about that city. That is your RAS at work.

The incredible news is that you can program your RAS to work on your behalf. Having a daily gratitude practice of finding new things to be grateful for helps you program your RAS to look for something to be thankful for the next day, the trick being to insist on new, keeping it fresh and very specific each day. In effect, when pondering "Who am I?" as this chapter suggests, you can take control of the person you are becoming by programming your RAS to look for things you find valuable.

Before moving on to the exercises, let your desires guide your self-discovery journey. Guaranteed, you'll find more beauty and fulfillment when you do. Again, this essential point must be made, it is okay to want what you want. The desires I am talking about are aspirational, which touch on improvements to your life, relationships, and work.

For example, if you want more time in life to read for pleasure, more sex with your consenting romantic partner, or better pay and more vacation time, those are healthy, normal, positive urges that you should be able to discuss. For work-related desires, dig into those now. For the other passions that are not work-related, I suggest that you navigate those conversations carefully and, where it makes sense, bring in professionals who can help you chase those desires in healthy ways.

A final critical component to discovering and defining who you are relates to how you show that person to the world. We are constantly being noticed by others, like it or not. Whether it is fair or not, others notice our activities, our distractions, and what sums up to be our work ethic. If you show up early and work hard, colleagues see that. If you show up late, take many breaks, look at your phone at your desk, and leave early, they see those things, too. Tilt the odds in your favor of positive judgment by others by being mindful of how you present yourself to the world.

In marketing terms, the question "Who Am I?" becomes "What is my personal brand?" with the natural corollary question being "What am I doing to protect my brand?" Being deliberate about how you come across to others and how you appear on social media and in your own published works translates into staying well-defined in the eyes of the public. The more you are defined and centered on a specific personal mission, the more potential employers can learn about you when you interview.

To connect all the dots from this chapter about discovering yourself, increasing your alignment with kindness practices, and then defining and protecting that brand to the world, below are exercises that will help. As you explore each exercise, remember that knowing yourself better allows you to engage your superpower of kindness more effectively for yourself and others.

CHAPTER 3 EXERCISES

Exercise 1: Identifying Inspiration

To make progress in life feel easy, almost effortless even, identify what inspires you. You probably already have a mental list of what drives you, like food, music, stories, travel, companionship, learning new things, or something else. Make that list concrete by writing down everything you can think of that inspires you.

It can be helpful to reflect on anything that has motivated you recently or garnered a comment from a friend or coworker regarding how energized you have been since some event.

Ponder any relationships with mentors, teachers, or adults you admire. List anything about those people and those relationships that have felt inspirational.

Whatever list you create in your journal now, your mission is to add as many of these elements into your daily life as possible. If you feel energized when listening to music, create and update playlists to hear that music. If you love hearing stories about successful disaster relief, find news sources that dwell less on the disaster and more on the successful support provided. If you find that a particular teacher believed in you and made you feel excited about life, use the lessons they taught to continue building the life you want.

With sources of inspiration cataloged and understood, take the final step: list ways of infusing those sources of inspiration into your workplace, your work tasks, and your career, and then do it. Use these new ideas to make your workplace *your* workplace. You might need alignment from your supervisor and colleagues to make them stick, so talk through your ideas whenever you feel it will help. For anything else, dive in and make your work more inspired.

Exercise 2: Creating a Compass for Your Life

While a compass points to a true magnetic north here on Earth, your life's compass points toward your ideal life. So, let's make one to keep you aware of where you want to go versus where you are headed at any moment.

If you prefer the written word to guide you, use your journal. If you are more visual, there are several tools you can use to put images in the forefront, including Pinterest and Microsoft PowerPoint. I suggest using Microsoft OneNote for those preferring a visual and written word version.

In your preferred medium listed above, create four categories:

1. Values and Beliefs

2. Life Goals (as far into your future as you can imagine)

3. Long Term Goals (within the next five years)

4. Short Term Goals (within the next year)

Values and beliefs are the ideas that guide why you act and how you act. If you believe running a pet store is the best fit for your life, the values could be "pets deserve good lives" and "pet owners need good resources to care for their pets." The belief could be that "pets have worth because they have feelings and need love just like humans do."

Life goals are the things you hope to accomplish during your life. While these could be work-related, they need more context than your career or specific jobs. If you wish to marry, travel, or create beautiful paintings, these life projects must be on the list. By starting with this list, you break down the steps needed across your lifetime to accomplish these big goals. With this list in place, it can be easier to know tasks that need to be done in the next ten days, let alone the next ten years.

Long-term goals are the steps you need to take to support your life goals. Long-term goals give you a sense of how to reach each life goal. Any long-term goal, like marrying, traveling, creating beautiful paintings, or opening a pet shop, will require more than good intentions. It will also demand knowledge and money. Each long-term goal could spawn several other goals or, at the very least, could be interdependent with other goals. An example would be owning a pet shop (goal one) requiring specific education (goal two), certifications (goal three), plus enough starter money (goal four) to afford rent on a building and starter inventory.

Short-term goals are the tasks or projects you need to do in the next year to support your long-term goals.

As you create your vision for your life, remember that your values and beliefs are like a compass showing you a reliable direction. The goals, be they short-term, long-term, or life goals, can take longer because of obstacles, your health and energy level, unexpected changes in employment, or other unforeseen circumstances. Your goals can just as quickly change because you achieved things faster than you previously thought possible.

CHAPTER 4
ASSEMBLING THE RIGHT CREW

E nvision the future, one in which we insistently pursue kindness in the workplace. Others take notice and join us, merging our efforts to build a kinder workplace, together. Along with these kindred spirits, we shine like beacons within our workplace, glowing with our good examples of inclusion, uplift, and collaboration. Those who would typically stand in opposition realize that their negativity cannot penetrate the protective force field that shields our local community. Those who persist in unkindness must either adapt to this kinder culture or find a new workplace.

People who learn our work culture across multiple businesses, leading with kindness in every interaction, catch hold of the movement and start chapters at their workplaces. Before long, the movement has momentum, and each participant claims ownership. The effort to lead with kindness grows beyond businesses, takes hold of the world, and makes it possible to see others as neighbors instead of enemies. Those who would turn us against each other have no standing, and the future we always wanted is suddenly here.

It all starts with two straightforward beliefs: you matter, and so do your actions. All you need to get started is a bit of bravery and the strategies in this book. Once you tap into the kindest part of your heart and try some daily exercises I will teach you, kindness becomes your default. It becomes your habit.

It can feel frustrating, even frightening, to pursue personal ownership of what happens around you because the news highlights outraged people who hurl profane insults while others cheer them on. You might feel outnumbered. Those who hurl insults are bonded to each other with outrage, their outward expression of pain and loneliness. It is exhausting, painful, and poisonous and either explodes or fizzles out as the outraged calm down and realize that anger and hate are unfulfilling.

Your kindness practice is the antidote. Genuine, heartfelt, simple acts of kindness build trust. It inspires others. It reminds you that even small, kind actions can lift others in ways that linger. You don't have to know or deeply love others to show them kindness. Creating and sticking to a deliberate kindness practice and cultivating your kindness superpower will inspire others and build deep connections.

When you believe, as I do, that kindness should be your guide in all your interactions, you naturally start attracting attention. You begin making friends who see your sincerity, share your optimism, and start to believe that they, along with their actions, matter, too.

No matter what you envision for your life, surrounding yourself with good friends who support your goals will significantly increase your odds of becoming the person you hope to be with the kind of life you wish to lead. The same idea applies at work. As you define and chase your career goals, your colleagues can become your allies as you pursue those goals. The trick is figuring out which colleagues are going to be those allies.

Creating your community at work means, at least in part, connecting with and deliberately staying bound to select colleagues during your career. Building this network means considering which people to connect with, learn about, keep in touch with, and periodically reach out to. Looking at networking from a more philosophical level, it will matter what kinds of people you include, either by deliberate choice or by circumstances you cannot control. By establishing a conscious approach to building this community, you will shape your career more effectively.

Consider how you build friendships now. Is it through trial and error? What rules do you have, spoken or unspoken, for strengthening bonds? How and when do you decide to exclude someone from your social circle? Once you thoroughly examine and understand these pieces, you can apply your ideas to creating work connections.

The most powerful tool I use in building my communities

in my personal life and at work is the concept of your Core Five.

Motivational speaker Jim Rohn says, "You are the average of the five people you spend the most time with." Even if you choose four or six, this group of closest, most trusted colleagues at work is your crew. Research supports the idea that if your innermost circle of colleagues, friends, and family smoke cigarettes, your chances of becoming a smoker increase. If any of your five closest friends work out and eat healthy meals, you will likely make similar choices. There are no guarantees that surrounding yourself with studious friends will give you better grades, but it does increase the odds that your study habits will improve.

Here is the mind-blowing part–this goes at least two levels deeper. The research shows that choices made by friends of friends (*second-degree friends*) and even their friends (*third-degree friends*) measurably affect your health, the choices you make, your likelihood of wealth, and even your lifespan.

If you have ever heard someone speaking in worried tones about a relative who "runs with a dangerous crowd," fearing that they are likely to engage in some mischief, research indicates that there is good reason to fear for that relative's safety because they will be more likely to make unsafe choices. While it is not fair to accuse someone of misdeeds or crimes based on the company they keep, it is reasonable to assume that the company any of us keeps is likely to influence us.

What about the workplace? Aren't we stuck with who is

around us as we work?

Fortunately, we have several factors in our favor in the workplace.

The most apparent factor working in our favor is that we select where we work. If you choose to work at a company that aligns with your beliefs and aspirations, that is likely to be where others have similar beliefs and aspirations. Working for an aerospace firm focused on sending the first humans to Mars increases the likelihood that you will encounter colleague after colleague who genuinely believes humans should venture to other planets. If that is your passion, you should do what you can to work there. Choosing where you work dramatically increases the chances of working with at least a few like-minded individuals.

Second, most companies have codes of conduct, sometimes called core values or workplace values, posted on their internal or external websites. These values could even be printed out and posted in various places around your workplace. This informs people that *anyone working where we work must adhere to these basic codes of behavior*. Have you familiarized yourself with those codes? Are your values aligned? It would be odd for someone who clashes with those values to persist in working there, though you can see that happen.

Assuming you align with your company's values, befriend those acting within those good behavior codes. I further suggest that you model good behavior for those who struggle to stay within those guidelines. When a colleague makes poor choices in conflict with your corporate culture, it will be far easier to offer them feedback and have hope of seeing changes if you've been behaving well.

Third, you control your behavior apart from any corporate value system. You can and should treat colleagues in thoughtful ways that model treatment you would like in return. When you ask someone how they are doing and genuinely listen to the response, you make it likely that they will want to hear how you are doing and support you when things are not going well. Little pieces of culture, like offering genuine praise for good work or asking your coworker about the sick relative they mentioned yesterday, can be powerful buoying forces to everyone around you. While you actively enrich your work community in these ways, you also can feel good about yourself.

The last factor working for you as you build the life you want and the network to support it is that you can control other variables about your work. As much as possible, decide the hours you contribute to work each week, select a good location for your workstation, ask for the projects you want to work on, and so forth. If you work hard and want to be effective, a good supervisor will work with you to increase your chances of success. With a willing supervisor at a healthy company, you have good odds of getting small wins that make you happier, thus, becoming a better colleague.

What if you have less kind, or downright toxic, colleagues? To handle toxic coworkers, start by modeling good behavior yourself. Recall my lousy behavior when I chose to badmouth my boss? It backfired, leaving me feeling shame and guilt even years later. Please avoid that pain for yourself and act in ways that let you hold your head high. Interact with everyone around you in kind and uplifting ways, including these more challenging colleagues. I share more strategies for dealing with toxic colleagues in *Chapter 6: Invisible Forces at Work*.

The single most important thing to know about building the right work crew is this: your success is tethered to your teammates' success. The more you are aware of and aligned with the people around you, the more you lift each other. When you deliberately choose to align with their joy, pain, success, and failure, you improve the odds that you will lend the proper support to your teammates, and they can provide you with what you need.

When I worked as a computer programmer at a 29-employee company that worked with pharmaceutical data, it felt cozy initially but quickly soured. There was good training and a sense of collaboration during the first few weeks. Still, gossip and cliquish culture demolished my motivation. After two years, I told my manager I was leaving for another company.

I landed in an all-remote team with two other programmers, one in California and the other in New Jersey. The three of us were tasked with figuring out how to map biomarker data, something wholly new and different from typical data mapping. Working in a new cobbled-together home office, away from the previous company full of tangled and broken work relationships, I stared at my screen and pondered, "How can I make this better?"

We were building new work processes from scratch, and everything was new and somewhat overwhelming. I love organizational design and process design. I knew I could make things work, but only if I truly knew my teammates and earned their trust. I reached out to my new workmate, Bineyam, stating hopefully, "I know this is new for all of us, but I want you to know that I am here for you. We are either all in this together or else what is the point?"

Bineyam replied, "Yes! This is how we should be! I am glad we are on the same team!" His enthusiasm, warmth, and kindness left me crying all over my new keyboard. Bineyam's kindness snapped me out of the culture of my prior toxic workplace and into the present moment. A lightbulb went off. He had experienced toxic work culture as well, and suddenly our shared pain was the bond that helped us forge something new together. He had lifted me up with his validation. He understood my previous situation and I understood his. I wanted to be kind and to lift others up. So did Bineyam.

My statement about being "in this together" was my attempt to put on a brave front, a fake-it-till-you-make it statement of what I hoped for. When Bineyam responded in kind, that is when I determined that I would consistently focus on kindness as my guide. I wanted to be kind even if it meant that some would mock it as naïve, others regard it with suspicion, and still others respond with cruelty.

If even a few kindred spirits like Bineyam came along for

the ride, it would be worth it. When I found this new friend and determined that lifting others with kindness is what I am all about, I no longer felt alone.

For years, I had believed in what my parents and teachers had taught me, namely that being kind to others should always be our goal. Then, I had been counter-taught that always centering on kindness was too naïve. What if you encounter jerks? What if it is clear someone is willing to undercut you or spread rumors or abandon you for their own benefit?

Nelson Mandela wrote about the South African idea of *ubuntu* as "…the profound sense that we are human only through the humanity of others; if we are to accomplish anything in this life it will in equal measure be due to the work and achievements of others." I have thought about the spirit of *ubuntu* for years because of its profound implications on society and each of our lives. I think of *ubuntu* in simpler terms, that your pain is my pain and your joy is my joy.

When I stop to consider your hardships at work, like not getting a key assignment for a project you wanted, I can recall similar times in my own experience, feel that pain of yours, and better understand and support you. And, if and when I must fight for others, my strength amplifies when I see, understand, and truly feel the pain they feel.

The same applies to joy. When you win an award that I did not, I find genuine joy in your happiness because I know how much that award means. My life is somehow richer for the knowledge that joy arrives in the hearts of others about whom

I care a great deal.

How can the concept of *ubuntu* help you in your work situation? How did it help me in mine after I met Bineyam? Before we get to that, let us dig into the science behind *ubuntu* and how it works within society.

Author and Harvard professor Shawn Achor researches the science of positive psychology and the factors that make people successful. In several of his writings, he notes that teams are far more successful when one factor—and one factor alone—is present: psychological safety.

Essentially, when people feel they can be open, honest, and fully themselves within a work team without worry that they will be harmed for doing so, the team thrives. As long as there are competent people on the team and everyone trusts in each other, they feel psychologically safe and do much better work. One example of this is Google's Aristotle Project, a giant project where they assembled and then evaluated their teams for factors that made them successful. The outcome conclusively showed that teams with psychological safety were more effective than teams of "all stars" who trusted each other less and did not communicate as well.

What this means for you is that if you act and behave in kind ways, truly embracing *ubuntu*, and your teammates align with that same philosophy, it results in psychological safety; and thus, a stronger and better team.

If you surround yourself with great communicators and endeavor to communicate well with your workmates, lift them up with joy, comfort them through pain, celebrate team successes, learn together through failures, share honestly what you think, and return to a default of a positive, growth mindset, the team has the best shot at soaring. So do you as an individual.

CHAPTER 4 EXERCISES

Exercise 1: Your Five

In this exercise, you will list out your most trusted, most supportive, most aligned work colleagues and write notes about them. This exercise is analytical in nature and can feel at odds with the emotions you have for the people you list. Further, the notes you take during this exercise could be sensitive and you should guard them well.

In steering your life, you must consider the nature of your friendships and kinships plus the impacts that each can have on your life's course. Similarly, in considering your career trajectory, you must consider the nature of the connections within your network. If your closest colleagues bring positivity, support, humor, and joy into your life, then this exercise should be straightforward. If, however, you're already worried, trust that instinct. It is *because of* those colleagues in particular that have immediately sprung to mind that you really, truly need to do this exercise.

Step One: In your journal, list out as many colleagues that you have in your current company and any others who stand out from prior jobs you have had. These should be connections who have the power to influence your projects, your daily work, or other aspects of your career. They could be someone who stands out in your mind because they always greet you in kind ways even though you don't usually have much opportunity interact otherwise. Take no more than ten minutes for this step.

Step Two: Next to each name, create three columns: Positive Impacts, Negative Impacts, and Bring Closer.

Under Positive Impacts, rate, from 0-5 how big the positives are from this person. A five means powerfully positive impacts on your work life (or positive intent/potential for those kinds of impacts), 0 means zero noticeable positive impacts, and the numbers between give you flexibility to put more or less weight to that person's positivity.

Under Negative Impacts, rate the negative impacts from that colleague in similar fashion with 5 being powerfully negative impacts and 0 being zero noticeable impacts.

Under Bring Closer, you have the chance to rank how interested you are in exploring a connection with this colleague. If you feel compelled to include this person as a network connection, rate this category as a 5. If you feel zero interest in including this person in your network, rate this category as a 0.

Total the points for each colleague using this equation: Positive Impacts rating minus Negative Impacts rating plus Bring Closer rating.

Example 1: Gerald is a teammate who treats you well much

of the time, but sometimes interrupts you in meetings and takes credit for joint work. You are not particularly close, and you have little desire to get closer. You might rate Positive Impacts as 3, Negative Impacts as 4, and Bring Closer as 0 for a total of $3 - 4 + 0 = $ **-1**.

Example 2: Your supervisor is always busy, but somehow manages to get you good projects and tells others about your great work. While you wish you could get a better performance rating during annual performance reviews, the ratings are never terrible. For your supervisor, you might rank Positive Impacts as 4, Negative Impacts as 1, and Bring Closer as 4 for a total of $4 - 1 + 4 = $ **7**.

Example 3: An informal mentor from your last job has kept in touch, listens carefully to you regarding current work struggles and helps as a thought partner. You might rank Positive Impacts as 3, Negative Impacts as 0, and Bring Closer as 5 (because you thoroughly trust and enjoy this connection) for a total of $3 - 0 + 5 = $ **8**.

Final Step: Create a new list of your network connections with the highest scores at the top, lowest scores at the bottom. Consider the top of the list in particular and list ways you can help support, sustain, and grow those connections. How can you make those connections life-long connections? Consider the bottom of the list and write down ways you can improve them. Realize that sometimes the best way to improve a bad connection is to distance yourself as much as possible from that connection.

In no way do I advocate throwing relationships away. There is room for us to spread kindness even to those who are unkind to us. It is imperative, however, not to fool ourselves. We have to approach relationships that are toxic in clear-eyed fashion. By continuing to treat toxic coworkers with kindness, we lose energy at each engagement, and we gain no ground if that person is stubborn. So, create distance between yourself and those toxic others. Be too busy working with those who give you uplift to spend time with those who would drag you down.

Exercise 2: Creating Your Network Tracker

We have a multitude of applications that can hold contact information for you as you build your network. You will weigh that network's worth more fully with each passing month and each new entry. Knowing how valuable it becomes over time, preserving your contact information needs to remain a high priority throughout your career. Don't risk losing your contacts when the newest technology overwrites something in your records. Keep backups in different applications so that when one gets corrupted, you can find a new place to store backups.

You can track your network with something as simple as a contacts section within an email application, such as Contacts within Gmail, Outlook, or in an application on your mobile device. I cannot stress sufficiently how important it will be to have the ability to access and transfer that contacts list multiple times during your career, so choose wisely. The nightmare scenario is that a hardware glitch or software update obliterates your latest contacts which might also be your most critical ones. You are wise to preserve your contacts list as if each contact is worth a year of earnings. Even if you are only right about one out of 100 contacts, wouldn't it be critical to you to make sure you save that one contact's information?

Each time you meet a new colleague, take three minutes to record the following in your networking contacts application:

- Their name

- Their contact information

- Their family details (spouse, children, parents, pets)

- Details that make this contact unique (same college you went to, same home state, shared love of a hobby)

- How and when you met this contact

- What this contact has offered to do on your behalf in the past

    o Act as a reference during job hunting

    o Brainstorm with you as a safe thought partner

    o Connect you to other potential contacts with key support capabilities

- What you can do, or have done, for this contact. Be sure to include timelines.

    o Provide them information

    o Introduce them to a colleague

    o Mentor them

    o Act as a thought partner

When creating new entries for your network, it can feel constructed and contrived to list the names of the pets or family members of a new contact. Fight through that feeling by remembering that you value the new contact enough to take notes so that you can better support them, understand them, and connect with them. Remind yourself that recording details about your colleagues and friends is your way of supporting yourself in the future when a detail otherwise slips away from you.

CHAPTER 5
GROWING AT WORK

Have you ever started a new task with the thought, *even though I've never done this before, I'm going to be great at this!*? Then you try it, and you make mistakes. You get things wrong. Maybe rather than admit it, you double down, refocus, and try to muscle your way through.

We've expected too much of ourselves (another act of unkindness) ever since childhood. The first time we pick up a guitar, we think we should be able to play cover band quality hit songs when we jam. Expecting too much is the idea that we can cook a four-star meal following a recipe when we've never cooked before. In the back of our minds, we're putting all this pressure on ourselves (yet another act of unkindness), telling ourselves we have to wow people right out of the gates. On top of that, we do it solo. We don't ask for any help. We think we have to do it all by ourselves, no matter how lost we feel.

That is pride, my friend.

Ego.

Imagine you show up to your first week of work with this attitude. You pump yourself up thinking *they hired me for a reason. I can do this.*

Then, you try some tasks in the new job and find that you make mistakes because of how little you know. Then, pride and ego take a back seat to fear.

You couldn't just do the work and have everything turn out perfectly on the first try. *They hired me for a reason* quickly turns into *Oh no! I'm a fraud!* Even worse is when a new coworker notices or says something, and you can't tell if they are poking fun at you or trying to be encouraging.

What is the cure for all of this? How can we eliminate the pain, fear, and worry?

Get a mentor.

When you think about it, you have a coach the first time you try out for a sport. The first time you try out an instrument, you have a music teacher. You have apps, books, videos, and a teacher when you learn to speak a new language.

When you start a new job, why not take the time to find a mentor? A great mentor can do two things for you. First, they can help you figure out a path to becoming the best you can be. Second, they can save you from your own worst impulses.

Growing up, I was privileged to the point where I didn't even realize I needed a mentor. Most people who interacted with me wanted me to succeed, saw paths for my success, and helped me get from one milestone to the next. These were volunteer, stand-in mentors. Kind people who realized I needed a nudge and gave it.

When I started in the working world, I didn't recognize the need for a mentor or the benefits I could get from one. I assumed that, like in school, leaders would automatically look to everyone they supervised and take it upon themselves to help us. I didn't recognize that leaders at my work already had excessive work to keep them occupied, plus they weren't mind-readers. They wouldn't know that out of the ten people reporting to them, I wanted time and attention to improve my skills.

Like anyone in my situation, you can see how I needed a mentor, right? I did, after all, have shame-filled work moments, like when I faced my boss, Terry, after he found out I was actively working to undermine him. In retrospect, violating my values to undermine my boss was clearly a terrible strategy. I knew how I handled that situation would haunt me for years. But, the worst part? I felt utterly alone.

What about the time when my coworker Angie and I became friends, then colleagues gossiped, saying a romance was brewing? When she bailed on our friendship, things got so weird that I had to find a new workplace. Even though I wasn't actively violating my values in this new workplace, I had another job exit to plan. This time precisely what had gone wrong was unclear. I felt alone again.

Looking back on these situations now, where feeling alone was essential to my discomfort, one thing could have made a difference—having a mentor.

With a mentor, I could have devised a strategy for communicating with Terry that brought more alignment. I could have crafted a better response by understanding Terry's concerns and goals and not focusing exclusively on his flaws.

Regular meetings with that mentor could also have provided my mentor with insights about my workplace where Angie and I became friends. He could have asked the now-obvious question: Have you been expanding your network in *other* ways at this new job? With that single prompt, I might have invited other key teammates to lunch and gotten to know them. I might have diversified my time, giving me a few other connections to focus on. It would have given gossipers less fuel for the fire that eventually burned my situation to the ground.

Most of us don't realize that mentors hide in plain sight. You might be a bit stunned to find out: I already had a great mentor that whole time and just hadn't realized it. Let me set the scene for you and show you how I found him so that you can avoid the mistakes I made.

At the start of my sophomore year at UNC, I walked into Morehead Planetarium hoping to secure a job. A friend worked there as a student employee and encouraged me to apply, so I figured trying couldn't hurt. A few years earlier, I had gone to this same planetarium with my visiting aunt, uncle, and cousins. During the show, stars appeared on the large, curved surface above our heads, making it seem like the stars had somehow burst through daytime to reveal themselves. It looked and felt spine-tinglingly real. I felt awed by the star projector sitting in the middle of the 68-foot diameter dome, looking like an enormous space satellite that had crash-landed in the middle of the cavernous space.

Would I really get the chance to work in that dome and use that machine?

A middle-aged man greeted me with a hearty handshake, saying, "Michael Neece, so good to meet you. I'm Jim Horn. Let's go upstairs and talk." He led me up the curving, green-carpeted spiral stairs adorned with brass handrails. As I walked through this luxurious space, I wondered aloud why it was so beautiful. Jim responded, "John Motley Morehead the Third," the man after whom the planetarium was named, "was a wealthy man. He wanted to give North Carolina something truly special."

Sitting with Jim Horn for the next hour, I wondered if I would work with him. I didn't know how jobs worked, so I thought perhaps the initial interview would be with someone random. Of course, Jim was interviewing me because it was his first opportunity to look over recruits into his student employment program.

He was so warm and welcoming. I was compelled by his ability to weave beautiful stories together even while asking me about my hopes for employment, my background, and skills, and telling me how he expected employees to act. As I left the planetarium that day, my interest in learning about star patterns and working in the dome was eclipsed by wanting to work with a supervisor who felt like a treasured uncle.

Little did I know that Jim Horn would continue to be the

yardstick against which I measured my supervisors. One year into working with Jim, he made me a shift supervisor. His great advice was to check in with the other students to ensure they had what they needed, felt they knew what to do, and knew that I was there to support them.

Two years into the job, I became chief technical student supervisor. Jim taught me about emergency situations, how to keep audiences calm during a power outage, and what to do if the fire alarm went off. We went over not just emergency procedures but also technical procedures and how to teach others about the vast control system we used to present star shows.

Three years into working my part-time job at the planetarium, another student missed shifts, showed up late, and started to drag audiences into his world through depressing monologs. During one of his show introductions, he told the audience how depressed he was, that he had overextended his credit cards, and that living life was like "being in the innermost circle of Dante's *Inferno*."

This was when Jim became much more than my supervisor–he became my full-out mentor. He treated me as a partner in the discussions about how to help, or possibly fire, this student. It was then that I learned the most essential principle of the workplace, a principle I have had to reteach myself a few times: always empathize with your coworkers and give them as much kindness as you can regardless of what actions you take.

Jim always showed curiosity about the context that may have led students to make poor choices. Every time he and I met, we discussed how the students under our care were do-ing. He knew them all by name and recalled details about them. Jim dedicated himself to keeping records about each person who worked for him. At first, this seemed to me like a potentially tedious and unnecessary activity. Why track details about those in his care?

A couple of other difficulties arose while I worked with Jim, testing just how deep his mentorship was because it was in those moments when we had to make hard decisions about the students we fired, and other students who needed some discipline, that I finally understood. Jim really wanted to make sure he got the details right because every single person in his care mattered to him. He never shied away from making tough choices; however, he executed them with compassion and empathy, which made all the difference.

We navigated difficult waters together, such as when I asked Jim to confront another division head who deliberately excluded Black and other minority candidates when hiring. I also asked Jim to help me file a complaint about a supervisor who sported an inappropriate bikini calendar in a workspace. When we con-versed about these issues, Jim listened more than he talked, then assured me he would handle them. When I saw changes made to the workplace, like Black employees being hired and trained and the bikini calendar removed, I knew he valued honest communi-cations and took workplace harmony seriously.

We did have our moments of disagreement. In one in-stance, I took it upon myself to go above and beyond. Jim reminded me of my father, and I wanted to impress him. I saw a gap in our training where I had stumbled through things, and I wanted to help the newcomers. To remedy the training problem, I created a series of guidebooks to help students learn their roles better and consequently find better approaches to work. It felt helpful and appropriate to me, but when after two weeks of work, I presented the guidebooks to Jim, he didn't see value in them. He reminded me that he made his expectations known to new hires in conversation. "But, but, but," I protested feeling insistent my way was the right way, and a little hurt that I wouldn't get the chance to express my gratitude to Jim by doing more than he'd asked. Ultimately, though he remained calm and kind, he said the decision was his to make. Though it took me a while to get over my bruised ego and my feelings of righteousness, in retrospect, I realize, even then, in the midst of conflict, Jim was teaching me boundaries using kindness as his guide.

That wasn't the only time I was fascinated by Jim's ability to create and uphold boundaries while also showing me he was on my side. When I missed part of a shift and finally showed up out of dress code, he made sure I understood I could not do that again, but that he sympathized with the reasons I was late to work. My girlfriend had broken up with me earlier that day and I was so despondent, I forgot all about work. It wasn't until the person covering my shift called to ask if I was coming in that I even remembered.

Empathy and kindness, and many other learnings from my

time with Jim, have become integral parts of my own supervisory practice. Why hadn't I leaned on Jim during those other situations that arose in later jobs? The simple answer? I hadn't fully processed Jim's offer to lean on him later in my career. He was always there, easily within reach. I just never reached for him because I didn't think of him as my "mentor." I was too worried I would be an imposition on him rather than realizing that Jim truly cared about me, no matter where I worked.

So, what about your mentor? Can you easily identify at least one? If not, how can you identify the right mentors?

First, let's define what a mentor is. A mentor is someone with deeper experience than your own in a profession or in one or more areas where you desire growth. This person will happily guide you as your career unfolds. They should be interested in your success, share ideas that help you, such as insights, wisdom, and feedback on how to improve what you do.

When seeking that more experienced partner in your career development, key characteristics to look for include someone who is trustworthy, willing to make time for you, and interested in seeing you excel. To get the most benefit from that mentor, you should know or strongly suspect that you can hear their feedback in the spirit it is intended—as information to help you, not as a glorification of how wrong you can be. When you can digest and understand feedback, you can put it to use in your growth and learning. Finding the right mentor can be tricky based on a multitude of factors, but using a checklist can help.

The most important quality of any mentor is that they align well with your values and beliefs. If a potential mentor treats others kindly in public and in private, and they do not speak ill of others or share private information about anyone else with you, that is generally someone worth considering. A potential mentor who has a string of broken relationships in their life could be a good mentor, but this fact could be a red flag, indicating that the mentor acts from different motivations than you do or perhaps makes different calculations than you do when making decisions. A good choice for a mentor should be someone who feels trustworthy and who makes you feel safe.

A second important quality is that the potential mentor is more experienced in some way. Perhaps they have previously been in similar roles to your own. Perhaps you admire how they handle certain situations, such as interactions with their leaders, oversight of projects, and supporting their supervisees (called *direct reports*). When you see the potential mentor consistently doing a set of activities in a way you consider admirably or efficiently, weigh that in their favor.

A third quality is that the potential mentor fits you during this season of your life. When I was a teenager, a brilliant martial arts instructor named Jewell Allen took me under his wing and taught me about resilience, hard work, excellence, and persistence. While I will forever be grateful for the instruction and mentorship I got from him, he fit in my life as a mentor during that season of my life, but not since. Even though he is not currently my mentor, I still benefit from the principles and ideas he taught me. Thinking of that era in my life as a season helps me maintain perspective on the role of that mentorship in my personal history and its lasting impact on the person I've evolved into over time.

The exercises at the end of this chapter will give you concrete ways of analyzing your current network to identify a good mentor. If you get to the end of the exercise and find that your pool of possible mentors is not yielding good options, it may be worthwhile asking someone in your pool of candidates if they can think of someone who would be a good fit for you. You can also reach out to friends and family members to get leads for possible mentors. Don't hesitate to meet potential mentors a couple of times to see if there is a good fit.

Besides a mentor, what other colleagues become pivotal in your career progression? How can kindness help you build trusting, resilient relationships along the way?

Late in high school, I started taking martial arts lessons with some friends. Flash forwards a few years, and I was one of the trusted trainee instructors teaching taekwondo at Jewell Allen's Chapel Hill ATA. I taught several afternoons per week for kids let out after school and then for adults later in the evening. While my favorite part of taekwondo was being directed by Mr. Allen to improve my techniques, teaching felt like an extension of my soul.

Many memorable and skilled students came through the taekwondo school, and one really stood out: Erik Neill. He was a blond 11-year-old who learned fast, practiced at home a lot, and brought the energy of the modern-day Naruto to every class. His parents invited me over a few times, and I would occasionally drive him home. I introduced him to They Might Be Giants, and we sang along as I pulled to the curb to park and walk him inside.

Many years later, I was in a very different season of life and had not done martial arts for years. I was astonished when Erik called me, asking, "Are you the Michael Neece who used to train me at Allen's Taekwondo?" He invited me to work out with him at his progressive-style taekwondo studio.

Before I knew it, I had signed up to learn a new style of taekwondo from Erik—now *Master* Neill. It was only possible because our mutual goals of enjoying martial arts was also layered with friendship and mutual respect. I felt great pride in this amazing former student-turned-professional. I struggled against my ego reminding me that perhaps staying in training could have let me *stay* the teacher instead of becoming the student. Erik persisted in being welcoming, caring, funny, and so whiz-bang *amazing* at the art that my ego took a back seat to my affection for him and the excitement that I had more to learn from a trusted friend.

It is worth saying–as you progress through working life, you will make choices that leave certain possible futures behind on the path you walk. You can lament the what-ifs, but if you dwell in them too long, you will find yourself wishing away all of the good things that have happened since those decisions.

I am glad I studied taekwondo as a high school and college

student. I am forever grateful that I learned how much I loved teaching through this rigorous and fun sport. I am also thoroughly glad that I never pursued it as a profession since it would have choked off all the adventures and opportunities I have gladly taken since then. It was kindness that guided me through my exit of taekwondo during college as well as my return to it years later, learning from my former student.

Back to the idea of having the tables turn, which is a good possibility during the length of any given career. When the teacher becomes the student, or peers rise through the ranks and take on roles with higher titles than yours, I encourage you to lean into the spirit of *ubuntu*, immersing yourself in the joy of your colleagues and friends to celebrate their triumphs. When you can imagine roles being reversed, you know you would want them to wish you the best in your career advancement. Be kind to them.

When others rise through your company due to preferential treatment instead of legitimate grounds—or perhaps it is hard to understand those grounds from your perspective—it can feel much harder to follow *ubuntu*. Perhaps, they get promotions and better opportunities because of unconscious biases that favor groups of people, typically rewarding men and white people over others. It could even be as simple as personal relationships between those who give out the promotions and those who are getting promoted. As you see others moving up in the corporate world and suspecting you have been overlooked, it feels like a gut punch. How can you press forward in productive and healthy ways?

Regardless of why someone gets a promotion and you do not, there are several strategies for handling these situations. What can be effective is working to raise awareness of the amazing qualifications of those who were overlooked, not in an effort to undercut the newly promoted colleague, but as a consistent effort to get these qualified colleagues the recognition they deserve. When we sing praises of those around us consistently, especially those who state that they dislike lifting themselves up because "it feels like bragging," you help increase the odds that one day your new supervisor will be one of these highly qualified colleagues.

If it appears that colleagues get promoted based less on skill and expertise and more in alignment with systemic bias, it is important to work with employee resource groups to make sure that the bias itself is called out. A word of caution: complaining about specific instances involving individuals who got promoted over you will seem petty. You will be called out for jealousy instead of logic, even if jealousy had nothing to do with the complaint, and you could be stuck with a "sore loser" label. It can even harm your relationship with that newly promoted person who, whether they are more or less deserving, holds greater power than they did previously. The strategy of pointing to the bias instead of the individuals involved may feel less satisfying in the face of injustice, but it is far more effective.

If you find yourself in a position where you long for promotion but you feel like you are not advancing while others do, there are options available to you. Seek feedback from decision-makers about what you could do to strengthen your resume and to make a better case that you are ready for those greater responsibilities. If you receive feedback that you need more education or more experience, ask your supervisor for work that will show off your skills and talents. Seek professional development that your company likely offers, usually with some budget available to assist your efforts. Research what tuition reimbursement programs might exist at your company and determine if a certificate or college degree program would be interesting to you. Earning more credentials is always worth the investment when you learn. If they're valued by decision makers, that's the icing on the cake.

Here are a few quick notes that I suggest you honestly address.

MOVING UP

Do you want to move up?

If the responsibilities that go along with a promotion are genuinely exciting to consider, then the answer is likely "Yes." If you are happy working in your current role and the attraction to the potential new position mostly revolves around the higher salary, then the answer is likely "No." One of my dear friends, Drew Gilmore, prefers holding a second-in-command position wherever he goes because he can advise leaders, engage in the work he was trained for, and not be stuck making final decisions that might or might not be heralded by others. While being revered as a subject matter expert in the planetarium profession, an associate directorship suits his needs since it keeps him focused on the work he loves doing and keeps him out of budget meetings.

If you cannot say for certain that you wish to stay in *implementation* roles (where you carry out orders) more than leadership roles (where you determine what comes next), grow in ways that are appealing to you and see where it leads. It is better to be overprepared and follow your curiosity than underprepared for the day when you long to have more responsibility. Preferences evolve over time, so having solid leadership training can be helpful.

Will your current company allow you to grow over the next few years?

You can be in a terrific company aligned with your values, beliefs, and goals, and have insufficient growth opportunities. Alternatively, you could be at a company that is not a great fit in some significant ways but there are opportunities to learn, lead, and advance. Which one is better? Can you have conversations at the first company that produce new opportunities for you? Can you stick with the second company for long enough to advance and get experience, then move to another company in a higher role?

It is helpful to decide how long you want to be in a role or to get an idea of what indicators you need to see to know that opportunities are likely coming your way, on your timeline. As an early career employee, you may have to do a lot of less appealing tasks for some time so you can learn, get experience, and advance to more desirable tasks. These experiences are invaluable. If you can get an idea of what typical times there are for advancement, that can help you determine what feels okay for your own career.

When I was first learning taekwondo, I went from white belt to black belt in thirteen months. I did work hard to make that happen, and I had enough talent to pull it off. But, it didn't mean much that I had gone fast and beaten the typical timeline. Clearly, you have never seen me jump-kicking in a Marvel movie or working out with Donnie Yen and Jackie Chan. So, what felt like a brag-worthy accomplishment to me turned out not to be an important milestone to the rest of the world.

I bring that up to make the simple point: If you find out what the typical time is for advancement in a work role, beating that timeline is meaningless beyond what meaning you personally bring to it. If you want bragging rights, what can you exchange those for later? The answer is disappointing: the bragging will end up with colleagues rolling their eyes and whispering things about your ego. If you capitalize on that hard work by continuing with more hard work to get to a particular goal, then that milestone will soon be in the rearview mirror as you achieve new things.

I will give you another story from my career involving turning tables, this time with a trusted and kind-hearted supervisor who eventually joined a team where I became his supervisor.

In my early days as a computer programmer, I had a supervisor named Derek Campbell. He hired me three different times, always encouraging me to seek better roles in the industry and always welcoming me back. Although we rarely interacted socially, I knew he respected my work when he told me before he hired me the third time, "As long as there's breath in my body, I will always find a job for you."

As great as Derek was at supporting me, he disliked managing people. Rarely did we have team meetings and the only one-on-one meetings we had were driven by project needs.

While I enjoyed the type of work I did for Derek, I eventually left for another company where I would have a chance to build a programming team. Derek expressed interest in joining my team, which took me by surprise, but I promptly welcomed him aboard. Over the first few weeks working together, he took me aside and said, "I will always be happy to offer you my perspectives, but I never want to 'run the show' again. Managing people is not something I enjoy, but you are a natural."

Derek fit in well with the team. He excelled at programming and provided excellent customer service to the data managers and other programmers who needed our reports and data sets. He helped recruit amazing teammates to join us from our old company. True to his word, Derek gave me his thoughts on one or two situations when asked, but otherwise steered clear of offering advice or critiques about my leadership.

When you encounter colleagues, supervisors, or supervisees, trust that at least once in your career, you will have a role reversal. When those tables turn, and you suddenly report to a supervisee-turned-supervisor, it serves you well to have a positive relationship ahead of time.

Fear of your subordinate suddenly becoming your supervisor is not a good reason to treat that subordinate well right now. It is the genuine warmth and kindness that makes your time working with that colleague and everyone else around you far more enjoyable and uplifting. The side effect of that authentic set of kind interactions is that you will never worry about encountering a colleague from three jobs ago when they are hired to be your new supervisor.

The exercises below get you to think about potential mentors discussed at the beginning of the chapter, strategies for your own career growth, and strategies for how to handle role-reversals with genuine kindness.

Want help beyond the exercises below? Dig deeper at www.michaelgneece.com by downloading my free tips on finding a great mentor. Go even deeper by setting up a free call with me and we can start sorting it out together.

CHAPTER 5 EXERCISES

Exercise 1: Identifying Your Mentors

Similar to the activity in Chapter 4: Assembling the Right Crew, in this exercise, you will list out your most trusted, supportive, and aligned work colleagues and write notes about them. In this case, however, you are attempting to identify someone who is farther along in their career path than you. This exercise is analytical in nature and can feel at odds with the emotions you have for the people you list. Remember, the notes you take during this exercise could be sensitive, and you should guard them well.

In finding a mentor, you must consider the nature of your work relationships and the impacts that each can have on your life's course. If your supervisors and the seasoned workers at your workplace bring positivity, support, humor, and joy into your life, then this exercise should be straightforward. What you might find, though, is that some of your candidates for mentorship come from prior experiences, like previous jobs or school. Just because you never thought to put the label "mentor" on someone doesn't mean you should overlook them now.

Step One: In your journal, list out seasoned colleagues that you have in your current company, even those in other work groups, and any others who stand out from prior jobs you have had. These should be connections who have had the power to influence your projects, your daily work, or other aspects of your career. Note that they could be someone completely apart from your specific workflow, but stood out to you as special, knowledgeable, and kind nonetheless. They could be someone who stands out in your mind because they always interact with you in kind ways. Add the names of any teachers you have had who seemed genuinely interested in your success. Take no more than ten minutes for this step.

Special note: There is no need to list anyone who has similar or less experience than you do. You should only be listing potential mentors, which means that they have years of experience more than you do. One notable exception is if you have been in the workforce for 20 years or more, then it is worth looking at those who have made big gains in the working world as a more significant factor.

Step Two: Next to each name, create two columns—Positives and Negatives.

Under Positives, rate how big the positives are from this person from 0 to 5, where 5 means they understand your industry, the roles you aspire to, and have mastery of their own higher position; 0 means they are unlikely to provide anything you need in terms of advice and insight; and numbers between giving you flexibility to give weight to that person's positives.

Under Negatives, rate the negatives in similar fashion, with 5 meaning that they leave wreckage and disharmony in their wake; 0 meaning they are flawless in their kindness practice and don't appear to bring negative issues to a potential mentorship; and the numbers in between allowing flexibility in your rating.

Total the points for each colleague using this equation: Positives minus Negatives.

Special Note: If you expect that the negative impacts rating would be poor or if you have a gut instinct about a potential mentor that tells you not to list them, put them in a special list off to the side and indicate that they are not under consideration. If, at some point, you reevaluate them and they appear to have shifted toward the positive and your gut instinct has settled into a more positive feeling, reconsider. Until that time, be satisfied that you have other choices.

Example 1: Naomi is rising through the company fast, has great skills, and understands the work ecosystem in great detail in the areas you care about. She also treats others above her incredibly well, but those who report to her say she is not the best listener and does not foster growth. For Naomi, you might give her a Positives score of 4 and a negatives score of 3, leaving her with a total score of $4 - 3 = 1$.

Example 2: Your supervisor always stops to show you why things are being done. He solicits your input. Others who have reported to him for years really like his ability to listen, explain and motivate. For your supervisor, you might rank Positives as 2, Negatives as 0 for a total of $2 - 0 = 2$.

Example 3: Your college professor, Dr. Janeway, worked in your current industry for 25 years rising to a role five titles above yours. At school, she always showed deep interest in your progress and invited you to keep in touch. It has been a long time, but if you can step past the worry of being an imposition, this seems promising. You might rank Positives as 4, Negatives as 1, for a total of $4 - 1 = 3$.

Final Step: Create a new list of your potential mentors with the highest scores at the top, lowest scores at the bottom. Consider the top of the list and make an action list. Which great candidate do you reach out to first? It is always worthwhile having more than one mentor, but you will need to drive the conversations and the mentor-mentee relationship, so perhaps start with one, then build up to two or even three. Start by setting up a time with your mentor candidates and see how they "fit" you and your situation. Once the timing feels right, ask if they will formally take on the role of mentoring you.

Exercise 2: Keeping Your Mentor Close

On your primary calendar, create a regular check-in with the mentor or mentors identified in the previous exercise. This entry should have no end date, should be at least once per quarter and probably no more frequent than biweekly.

By sending a text, email, or having a regular phone, video, or in-person coffee date, you can remind yourself that you have a resource in the form of a mentor who cares about your career progress and probably about you personally as well. These check-ins can enhance the life of your mentor as well since as you gain experience and wisdom, you can be a sounding board for them as they navigate work choices as well.

What to do when your supervisee or peer becomes your supervisor?

1. Accept the situation. If you have feelings of envy or jealousy, make sure to cry it out, journal about it, hit a punching bag, or talk to someone you trust who does not work where you work. If you are happy about the promotion they got and don't have residual feelings about it, you will still need to accept the change, so anticipate what things will be like and what might change so you have fewer surprises.

2. Signal to your new supervisor that you understand the new relationship and that you will support them. Ask what kind of support would be most helpful so that it is clear to both of you.

3. Balance who they are now with who they were to you before the promotion.

   • If the supervisor was a friend prior to their promotion, continued closeness will undoubtedly be noticed by your peers. Understand that some perceptions are out of your control while also doing your best to avoid a relationship of favoritism.

   • If the supervisor was a colleague you had an antagonistic relationship with, avoid speaking negatively about their decisions, their new role, or other aspects of them that might aggravate you. As you genuinely support them, each good outcome or faithful attempt to support them will build trust.

What to do when YOU become the new supervisor?

1. Accept the situation. You have power and responsibility, take both seriously. Forfeiting any of the power leaves others without a sure-footed leader, while abusing that power leaves others less willing to speak truthfully about important aspects of work, so walk a fine line and get feedback from your new team.

2. If you have familiarity with some of your supervisees more than others, become a scholar of the ones you don't know as well and learn how to equally support all of those in your care.

3. Avoid playing favorites.

CHAPTER 6
INVISIBLE FORCES AT WORK

Imagine a colleague takes you aside and says that a mutual colleague cannot be trusted because they are "one of them," meaning something sexist or racist. How do you respond?

Confronting them may feel hard, even scary for you. Taking the issue to your new supervisor might get you labeled a troublemaker. Worse, you could nod and agree, get noticed by the insulted colleague who overheard you, and ultimately hate yourself.

In the small moments across a career, you stay on or stray from the path of integrity, that moral sense that you are honest and upstanding. Lots of leaders talk about how important it is to live and act with integrity. What many of them don't say is that the surest way to recognize where you are relative to that path of integrity is to stray from it. Yes, becoming as successful as you can be requires making mistakes. And, guess what? When you cut a corner or insult a coworker and feel deep shame and embarrassment your kindness compass is the one tool you can count on to navigate back to your deepest integrity.

As you navigate the workplace using your kindness compass, you can only guess what's happening beneath the surface for your colleagues. Making the right forward motion will inevitably come with making a misstep that lands you in questionable territory. You can have the best intentions and still find yourself in trouble. You could be kind to someone universally disliked in the office, then find yourself ostracized. You could interact with a new work friend in ways that feel painful to them, like wishing them a happy Father's Day when their messy divorce keeps them from their kids.

You had no idea! I know, that's how mistakes happen. What's more, just about every colleague will have issues that could set them off. It is impossible to tiptoe around enough to protect yourself and your colleagues from the invisible forces at work, theoretically protecting each person and the work culture at large in your office. So, how can you spot the invisible forces at work? What can you do to safeguard your livelihood? How can you continue to operate in stressful, change-filled moments while leading with kindness? How can you put the odds in your favor with all these invisible forces without making yourself crazy? Let's dig into it!

THE DANGERS OF IGNORING OR
NOT UNDERSTANDING INVISIBLE FORCES AT WORK

To learn about invisible forces that exist in any workplace, it is helpful to imagine that you are looking for a new job. What do you hope it will be? How can you get ready and anticipate the various undercurrents that might exist there? Examining these questions and doing easy research, you can learn much of what you need to know. Even better, you will be able to craft how you fit into that new role in a way that will likely get you noticed for all the right reasons.

Leading with kindness is extremely helpful because it builds trust; however, kindness without a realistic, deep understanding of the forces around you leaves you defenseless. If you try to macho your way through invisible forces, it is like trying to bypass security measures at a fancy museum. You will trigger silent alarms that others will notice, and only luck will govern if that problem is small or career-ending. If you want to get ahead and make fewer embarrassing mistakes while you do, learn about the invisible forces at work.

ONGOING HISTORY CAN CREATE UNDERCURRENTS

Imagine starting a new job. No matter the job, when you go in on day one, the story of your workplace is already in progress. You know that there are undercurrents, complete with stories of employees arriving and others leaving the company, processes and technologies that have evolved over time, conflicts and misunderstandings among the stakeholders, as well as ongoing relationships that were strengthened by the ups and downs of day-to-day business. Not knowing the subtext can feel dangerous, and disorienting, like a tiny misstep could trigger an explosion.

When I started as a trainer at a web hosting company called Genuity, I joined a team with a history. The industry was new to me, but I had high hopes because most of the team was kind and supportive. One undercurrent I stepped into was the conflict between my new director and the head of training, a contractor. One of the training contractors, Kiersten, worked diligently and kindly to bring me up to speed while the head of training avoided me. The other undercurrent? Kiersten and her training colleague were being phased out. In other words, I had been hired to replace them.

When I understood what was happening, I recognized how lucky I was to have Kiersten by my side, setting me up for success while remaining the consummate professional until the very end. Knowing she would leave soon, I felt lousy, but she reassured me she already had her next work gig lined up. Meanwhile, I could relate to the other colleague who wouldn't give me the time of day. He was closer to the end of his career, had gotten into heated disagreements at this job, and was given his walking papers and the request that he train his replacement—me. It had to be hard for him, worrying about finding a new job, supporting a family, and wondering how things had gone wrong.

While I didn't know these invisible forces initially, I had to learn them. I also needed to remember that I had done nothing wrong. Knowing about the undercurrents doesn't mean accepting blame for them. It means humanly, kindly addressing hidden realities as you unearth them, even while going about your business. It means acknowledging that there could be big feelings in the room, validating those, and pushing forward with common goals, empathy, and compassion. If you can stay alert, attuning yourself to new hidden realities as they surface, you will be years ahead of where I was in my earliest days in the workforce.

Once I started mastering my job and my predecessors left Genuity, a new undercurrent popped up. Vastly cheaper technologies than what Genuity provided to clients entered the market, and many clients started seeking those web service solutions. As this reality hit the company, the financial implications were felt. Genuity leaders had just expended lots of cash on two new, gloriously beautiful buildings, and revenue couldn't support the spending. Layoffs were next.

Fortunately, I could take my cue from Kiersten. Instead of being bitter or resentful while waves of my peers accepted severance packages, I researched potential new roles while finishing up the work that would help others once I was gone. Kiersten's persistent kindness throughout her exit inspired my ability to craft my own kind approach to my exit, something that might have been lost on me if I weren't paying attention and self-reflecting.

RESEARCH YOUR CURRENT AND POTENTIAL WORKPLACES

Finding gainful employment depends on industry shifts, evolving company strategies, personal relationships, and your background and skills. It also depends on how alert you stay for clues about when things might end. When something at work cannot be mended, having potential jobs lined up is critical for avoiding unemployment.

Backup plans don't always work, but having zero next moves can feel debilitating if things change on a micro level (like relationships) or a macro level (market conditions and new corporate strategies). When my Genuity layoff exit interview came, I happily took the exit package and moved to my next job without missing a beat. It could have been so much worse if I hadn't radically accepted what was happening, then explored and researched possible alternatives.

To avoid heartache and financial hardships, you need to become a scholar of the local and the global, the micro and the macro conditions that affect you. Starting at a macro level and zooming in, knowing about the industry you plan to join is helpful since companies typically have competitors and partners. Learn about the company you could work for since friends and families will start associating you with that company when you get the job. Research the site you are working at since companies expand sites, shut them down, or move them depending on market needs.

RESEARCH THE PEOPLE

Just as a company will vet you, running background and social media checks, before they give you an interview, you need to know about the people you are about to work with. Research the company leaders to see if you are aligned. Do your homework on these leaders to avoid being at the mercy of decision-makers who might act in surprising ways. Knowing more about these leaders in advance and asking trusted mentors and peers at your new job once you are there, is critical to your ability to advance and have a thriving career at that company.

Find out about the management and colleagues you will work with for 40 hours per week. Nobody wants to work with difficult people, so ask questions and look up backgrounds on LinkedIn.com. Last, learn everything you can about your position in the company, partly from how it was posted and primarily through the interview process. Ask who preceded you and why they left. If they left for philosophical reasons, that's a red flag, and you should ask follow-up questions. Leaving because they needed to move with their spouse, who just got a new job, may be fine. Ask what the job description says you will be doing compared with what is stated in the interview and listen for discrepancies. Human factors exist at all levels in a company. With that in mind, it is critical to understand more about human interactions and relationships.

ENSURE ALIGNMENT OF PURPOSE

When you apply for roles in your chosen industry, you will be more dedicated if your internal drive aligns with the industry's mission. You will have authentic answers when others ask why you work there. You must find an industry that aligns with your sense of purpose. It is easy to choose an industry that fights to build the future we want to live in. Look at people who do work that you admire and research where they work. Explore industries on LinkedIn or via an Internet search related to work that invigorates you. When it becomes apparent what work you wish you were doing, figure out what education, skills, and background you need for the roles you like best.

BE READY FOR THE INTERVIEWS

If you don't have all the prerequisites for a job role, don't let that discourage you from applying. It is worth applying if you have half or more of what they list in the job description. As an aside, men are generally more likely to apply to positions where they don't "check every box." Don't sell yourself short; apply anyway. If you get to the interview phase, be clear and honest about your experience. Add that you're a quick and eager study wherever you don't have experience. Many employers look forward to mentoring new talent, or justifying a lower pay grade. You can't know if any of that is the case before showing up for the interview, so give it a try!

If you truly have too few skills or educational credentials compared to the ideal role you have in mind, trust me when I say that it is better to apply to something—almost anything—at a company doing what you wish you could be doing. After all, wouldn't you rather work for a good company doing good work in a lower position than for a company that doesn't quite feel right doing something that doesn't matter to you?

A quick note about interviews: If you go through an interview process and eventually do not get the position, you could find out that a candidate who already works at the company is the favorite going in. Ask during your interview if there are any internal candidates for the role. That invisible force—being compared to an internal candidate—can be revealed simply by asking. In the event, that's the case, have great answers ready, highlighting the positives of bringing in your outside experience, perspectives, and skills. Remember, whether you get the job or not, interviewing is always an opportunity to build relationships.

For each follow-up interview, the interviewers want to see if you listened during the previous interview. They are likely also comparing your answers with those they got from other interviewees. Lean into who you authentically are, the traits that make you the kind of worker that might be precisely what they are looking for. Don't forget that they may want you to do deep research on topics to create a product you can present; or otherwise, wow them with the best of what you can do. Always bring with you genuine, warm, and carefully researched answers.

COMPANY FIT

If your preferred industry has visible public flaws that go against your code of ethics, such as well-known personalities who stand out for all the wrong reasons, it's essential to factor this into your job search. Consider whether there are companies within that industry that stand apart, where leaders have sterling reputations and employees are treated fairly. Choosing such a company could provide you with a refuge amidst the challenging industry conditions. Moreover, don't forget that a job is not a lifelong commitment. It's like a yoga pose; you don't hold it forever.

Read reputable online business news, like the *Wall Street Journal* and local online business publications. These can be key to knowing if your industry has promise or if you are jumping onto a sinking ship. The earlier you are in your career, the more industry longevity will matter to you. When I took on the web hosting job, I naively overlooked that newer technologies were already nipping at the heels of the company I would join. My interest in other industries was strong then, and I only needed to get a few years out of that job, so it worked out well in the end. The layoffs would have been a crushing blow, though, if I had been interested in a long-term position.

When considering a company you could work for, knowing how the industry views that company and its leaders can be critical. If leadership has changed at a company, where did the leaders previously work, and what were they known for at their old company? If a leader is known for trimming away the workforce, that leader is likely to do the same at a new company. By learning these trends, you can make the invisible forces visible before you make your decisions.

Another way that local newspapers and business journals can be helpful before you land that golden opportunity is by featuring stories about your potential new work site. For example, Bizjournals.com has news about what's going on in over 40 major cities in the U.S. If you know more about the relationship between the state and local communities, and the company you are hoping to work for, you might find out that the local site is under threat of closing, or perhaps it only just opened and signed a 5-year lease. Any details you gather will help you piece together the story before you invest time chasing an unstable job.

HOW TO RESEARCH POTENTIAL COLLEAGUES

Learn about your new manager and teammates by looking at LinkedIn.com. This can help you craft a cover letter and think of interview talking points. Like with all social media, you can get a sense of what your future colleagues do, what interests them, and how long they have been at the company. For instance, if many have long tenures at the company and advanced college degrees, that could be helpful information. Just like with all social media, know that you are seeing only a snapshot of highly-curated versions of. Still, hidden undercurrents you can't see can even be present in an online profile.

While doing your co-worker, company and industry homework will better prepare you, give you more confidence, and provide more talking points during an interview you still shouldn't make assumptions. Which colleagues will be on your team or what these future colleagues think about what you've read online are things you simply cannot know. Staying positive and being curious are your two best tools during these conversations and beyond.

Stay positive and curious even after you get the job. It is the best way to learn about your new managers and colleagues. The kinder you are at the outset, the more you set the tone that you are there to help, connect, and learn your new role. The signals you send in the early stages are critical to building trust and rapport.

Remember, human interactions and relationships are woven throughout all layers of your new employment. While it is impossible to anticipate the details of your workplace, some general rules apply.

WHAT LEADERS WANT

We often forget that any change made at work started with someone's decision. We don't intend it, but we often detach leaders from their decisions and guess that new things happen because of abstract forces. It is so easy to dehumanize our leaders, we forget that they are people who have worries, goals, joys, and fears. It is worth taking a moment to think about leaders and how changes at work are because of their thoughtful actions.

Leaders at your company are trying to guide and coach their employees to fulfill the company mission. Leaders at the top of a corporation are humans dealing with all kinds of high-stakes situations just like you and me, plus they're expected to carry forth the company mission.

While that mission could be spelled out on a company intranet, in an employee handbook, or on the company's website, leaders will also bring their needs and desires to the workplace. Rarely, if ever will they have the time to explain the nuances to you. Consider it a huge part of your job to know and care about the mission and how you can best support what your leaders are chasing. More specifically, carefully reading company emails drafted by leaders will give you insight into the individual focus of each leader.

Some leaders think of their work as a chess board with resources, budgets, and company goals as the game's pieces and the rules applying to their movement. From the moment you were hired, if not before, they've been considering where to place you for the most positive impact on their chess board. Maybe this seems impersonal to you, and depending on their proximity, and what they observe, and it may be. As a general rule, the closer you work with the leaders, the more likely it is they can see you as a human being worthy of kindness, attention, and support.

Consider carefully how you are noticed at your company. Do you show up on time, treat others with respect and kindness, and ask how you can help more when you run low on work? Colleagues and supervisors see that. If you show that you are helpful to others, perhaps that is valued. If you show off your skills, and leadership considers you powerful as a result, leaders in charge might move you to a different part of the chess board where you can carry out more significant parts of that leader's vision. No matter what happens, infuse kindness with others as you do your work, and your excellent attitude and leaders are more likely to give you the well-deserved credit for your attitude and work.

While you are making calculations on how to be most effective in your work, how to appear to others, and how to show off your skills enough to be noticed, remember that leaders have these same concerns.

Great leaders remember that you and your colleagues were hired because of your skills, knowledge, experience, and understanding of nuance related to some subject. They will foster a healthy environment in which you and your colleagues can freely exchange ideas and ask each other hard questions, always with the sense of trying to find the best path forward. Emotions will crop up, but great leaders will validate where you are coming from even if their final decisions don't align with your preferences.

FLAWED LEADERS

Leaders operating out of fear will have different considerations. Some might emphasize having their ideas pushed to the forefront, championing them even in the face of data-backed arguments for different solutions. Still others might overemphasize avoiding difficult conversations, claiming the desire to promote harmony even when a situation calls for staying firm with employees who refuse to align. Since these leaders are not leading from places that logically uphold the mission but from personal agendas instead, speaking up can be tricky. If you have a strong relationship with upper leadership, private conversations about your concerns about leadership misalignment with company goals might work. If you are in a place of lesser power and don't have those connections, understand that the orbits of the flawed leadership can be disjointed or even downright toxic. Fight for the mission, but consider your other options for employment since this split culture can affect your mental and physical health.

I have experienced both kinds of leaders. Once, I worked under a middle leader named Judith who wanted to replace our contractors with cheaper ones in another country. Even though Judith hadn't consulted with managers on the front line doing the work regarding what downstream impacts might result, she was adamant that we switch to the new model and had the authority to make the change.

Meanwhile, at that same company, a leader directly over

me named Eddie wanted to keep his direct reports happy and harmonious. Eddie insisted that if he treated all his direct reports fairly, they should each be allowed to do what they felt best rather than adhere to agreed-upon standards. The results, again predictable, were that each subgroup under Eddie created and carried out their versions of standards which were nonexistent in some cases.

When Judith and Eddie had to work together on offshoring the work, the lack of consistent, written standards meant resources and work tasks that were inconsistent and confusing. The work slowed even more, and both Judith and Eddie watched in horror as company morale descended and the best workers left for roles outside the company.

In short, leaders can be brilliant tacticians, self-serving egotists, or optimists who neglect realism. Knowing which kind of leaders you work with is critical. The exercises at the end of the chapter will help you score your supervisor and, by extension, any leader at your company.

A few last words about leaders: leaders will cultivate what they tolerate. Simply put, if a worker pushes away from the stated mission, goals, and established processes, letting that worker continue without enforcing the rules that everyone else is abiding by means that more workers will do the same. Leaders who think more about themselves—looking good at the expense of others, pursuing their ideas rather than the best ideas presented by experts on the team—will push others off the cliff if it means they can look good long enough to get a promotion or a jump to another company based on their initiatives. If things work out, they will quickly claim the credit, but if things go sour, they will blame others.

CULTIVATING POSITIVE RELATIONSHIPS WITH COLLEAGUES

You spend most of your time with colleagues. How can you make your experiences with them as positive as possible? Like you, colleagues mostly start with a desire to align with the company mission by doing work their supervisors asked them to do. As time wears on, however, some might feel out of place, lost, or even resentful of the workplace, the work, or their supervisor.

Knowing where a colleague is in their cycle of workplace engagement can help you align with those most enthusiastically engaged. Universally treating all colleagues *In Kind* is always your best bet. In time, you might find more affinity for some than others. It is healthiest to ensure you have many positive relationships rather than one or two deep ones since things could go sour and leave you without options.

Besides being an excellent philosophy for living and a great approach to others in your workplace, approaching others with kindness can serve a practical purpose: data collection. If you are kind to someone once and they repay you with kindness, you have an *In Kind* interaction of the best sort. Further, you have collected data about that colleague's tendency toward being kind. You can reasonably expect more kind interactions.

If you give kindness to another colleague and are repaid with sarcasm, anger, secrecy, being ignored, or something equally upsetting, now you have different data to consider. In either case, you can still exude genuine kindness. The first colleague who seemed inclined to mirror your kindness might have been putting on a front. In time, you'll know for sure. Similarly, if the colleague who was unkind, seems kind during your next interaction, maybe they were having a tough day.

Any which way it works out for you, I promise that if you keep dispensing kindness, you will learn more about the people around you. After being kind to someone several times in a row with negative responses in return, you can read that data and feel confident that they aren't just having a bad day. They are invested in toxic behavior and will rarely treat you with genuine kindness.

If possible, you want to avoid toxic behavior from colleagues, but you can still project kindness when you cross paths. As my mother-in-law always advises in these situations, "Kill them with kindness," meaning that you increase your positivity, especially when you don't want to. By avoiding caving in and resorting to fighting fire with fire, you give others nothing to fight against, so they cannot fling their troubling behaviors at you. You avoid their messes and remain true to yourself.

Your actions of paying others back *In Kind*, regardless of how they try to pay you, means you are maturing your kindness habits, keeping proper focus, and giving others a role model of positive behaviors. It is not a parlor trick–genuine kindness looks and feels a certain way, and most people can sense if you are being genuine. Your uplifting behavior makes you a reliable and safe person for others to approach honestly. This puts you into the minds of most colleagues and leaders in all the best ways, so everyone cheers on your success, wants to work with you if they can, and your name gets mentioned in back rooms when exciting new projects come up. The uplift is only a side benefit of being kind for the sake of being kind. What a great benefit!

Unfortunately, life at work can be messy. Difficult situations arise, and sometimes you need to tell or get told complicated truths. Can you adhere to kindness principles when someone shouts at you, ignores you, withholds information, or otherwise creates problems?

Absolutely.

Whether we know it or not, most of us value honesty. It is hard to come to a genuine understanding with someone who will deflect, defer, and otherwise avoid hard truths. Someone who tells us we have something in our teeth, that our zipper is down, or who thinks our approach on a project will not work saves us from difficulty or embarrassment. How can you receive those hard truths? How can you deliver them when you need to?

An excellent method for handling incoming information that could feel like an attack on your ego involves long, slow, deep breaths and assuming positive intent. The person delivering news that feels challenging to you can trigger a negative emotional response. That's why it makes sense to pause, and remember how brave they are in delivering the truth to you. Only someone who cares about you, or your mutual objectives, would offer up the truth. Assuming that they are not trying to embarrass you and instead trying to help redirect you can make all the difference in how you receive the news.

- When someone comes to you to deliver difficult feedback, I suggest a few handy phrases: "Thank you for telling me about this. I value your opinion and will have to digest this information for a bit, and then I might check back in with you."

- Or, "I was unaware. I can't say if I agree or disagree yet since I'm still just trying to process what you said. Can we talk more when I've had time to think about it?"

- Or, "Let me see if I understand what you've said correctly. I want to make sure I have it correct. [Repeat in your own words what they have told you.]" The exact wording is less important than the fact that you show you were listening, that you are attempting to process what you've been told, and that the emotions you might be feeling are not getting in the way of benefiting from what they've said.

- You can even say, "Wow. That's a lot for me to process on the spot. Can I think about this and come back to you with questions?" If you remember that the messenger is not attempting to harm you but instead help you with new information, it will make it far easier to process that information.

There are several ways of delivering hard truths depending on the recipient and how comfortable you feel with them. It is usually helpful to mention that you have feedback for them or want to tell them something that could feel challenging. Then, ask them how they feel about discussing what you have to share. That gives them a choice regarding when and how they hear the information. Once you are both ready to have the conversation, ensure it is in private. There are rarely any benefits to having a discussion in front of peers on topics that could challenge someone's authority or stir up strong emotions; instead, there are usually many downsides to sharing information publicly.

The question of how to deliver hard information should be answered with kindness and honesty. Here are a few rules that can help with this.

- Avoid "you" and "me" statements and use "we" statements when you can since this makes it feel more like you are facing challenges together and not singling anyone out.

- When you cannot avoid "you" statements, use language that precisely describes the situation, events, and observations without emotional language, such as saying, "When you interrupted others in today's meeting," rather than, "When you repeatedly butt into the conversation, drowning out other's voices."

- Last, and this cannot be emphasized enough, use curiosity as much as possible. Asking questions feels less like a threat and helps the recipient of your feedback feel like they have more control. It also helps inform you about things you might not have known, such as the lack of sleep at home due to a newborn or other things you can empathize with.

Some will dislike hearing feedback, but you will still need to give it. Suppose someone is making sexist or racist remarks. In that case, it is a minimum requirement to be a good ally by saying something like, "That makes me uncomfortable" or "I don't think what you said was intended to harm anyone here or reflects how you feel, so maybe you can rethink how you said that." If you are an ally, ensure those in the affected groups are okay with you speaking up rather than some other actions they might prefer. Also, make sure you understand your company's policies on sexism and racism so you can align with what are hopefully robust and reasonable policies.

Even if the message you need to deliver isn't as weighty as addressing a sexist action or remark, there will be times when feedback must be given. Other ways of delivering that feedback include something Kristen Hadeed calls the FBI method: Feeling, Behavior, Impact. Speaking of your feelings when a behavior surfaced and its impacts on your likely future actions might look like this: "I felt belittled and ignored when you talked over me in the meeting, and it makes me less interested in trying to talk in future meetings." Nobody can debate your feelings, so leading with the feeling is powerful. As for the behavior, if you describe it in non-emotional, accurate language, it can still be debated, but it gets the point across. As for the impact it has on you personally, it is not something any reasonable person should debate.

Giving others clarity is one of the greatest kindnesses you can do. There are likely to be emotions that arise, but handling those with kindness is also a sign that your kindness practice is mature.

Besides honesty, what else do colleagues want?

If a colleague is consistently lovely, hard-working, and reasonable, they probably want those things from you in return. These colleagues can be great allies in making company culture more robustly inclined toward positive, inclusive, mutually supportive interactions. A way to support and encourage them to stay in that mode is to give them kudos, either in person, by message, or by email. "Thanks for helping me on that task yesterday" or "How are you doing?" can go a long way.

Another colleague might feel more lost, not knowing what they need. For that kind of colleague, consistently including, complimenting, and supporting them is the best way to help them feel like they belong.

As for colleagues who seem inclined toward self-benefit at any cost or are unkind or even cruel, remember the rule that hurt people hurt people. Behind their actions could be several limiting beliefs, such as "there is never enough to go around," thus enticing them into grabbing all they can at whatever cost. It could also be that they were told that others could not be trusted or that they have real or imagined special status. Regardless of what limiting beliefs a hurt, angry, or domineering colleague might carry, these colleagues represent real risks to you. Other than repeatedly approaching them with supportive, kind actions and words, there are few actions to take regarding these colleagues. Try to determine what motivates them. The more you understand what worries them, what excites them, and why they do what they do, the more you can determine if the company mission and your philosophy allow you to help them on some projects. If so, help away! If not, it is probably best to steer clear of these colleagues when you can.

Regardless of how your leaders and colleagues show up within your corporate culture, remember that one general rule should always apply to your conduct: try to squelch gossip however you can. Part of dealing with others fairly and honestly is not participating in gossip. If colleagues want to include you in speculation about something involving other colleagues out of their earshot, simply stating that you don't like to talk about others when they are absent can cut the conversation short most of the time. If you hear trash talk about someone at the company, telling the gossipers that you hate speaking negatively about colleagues and would prefer to change the subject; this usually works.

When considering the invisible forces at work, there is no sure-fire way to know all of them, but you also don't need to. Understanding as many undercurrents as needed to avoid getting swept away is all you need to give yourself the best odds of dwelling comfortably in the culture.

In the following exercises, you can determine if your supervisor is giving you what you need, and you can rate the health of your workplace culture. There could be other factors in rating your supervisor and workplace, so feel free to include those as needed. Regardless, once you have used these tools to put your workplace into perspective, you should have a much deeper understanding of how and where you fit in.

TOOLS AND TAKEAWAYS

Survey: How Healthy is Your Workplace for You?

You can rate your workplace across various subjective measures in the following checklist. Take a moment beforehand to guess how positive your workplace is from zero (the worst imaginable) to 60 (the best imaginable).

Initial Guess Score: _____

If your initial guess score is shockingly different from the total derived from scoring all the questions below, that is worth exploring. Circle a single answer per question.

1. My company's mission aligns with my "why."
   (i.e. I am excited about what we do here.)

Strongly Disagree   Disagree   Agree   Strongly Agree

2. My pay is at least comparable to what others in this role in this industry get.

Strongly Disagree   Disagree   Agree   Strongly Agree

3. My colleagues recognize the excellent work that I do.

Strongly Disagree   Disagree   Agree   Strongly Agree

4. My supervisor recognizes the excellent work that I do.

Strongly Disagree   Disagree   Agree   Strongly Agree

5. The workplace culture is clearly defined.

Strongly Disagree   Disagree   Agree   Strongly Agree

6. The workplace culture aligns with my values and beliefs.

Strongly Disagree   Disagree   Agree   Strongly Agree

7. Bullies and difficult personalities are rare or nonexistent in my daily work life.

Strongly Disagree   Disagree   Agree   Strongly Agree

8. Kindness is a core characteristic of the culture here.

Strongly Disagree   Disagree   Agree   Strongly Agree

9. Gossip is rare or nonexistent here.

Strongly Disagree   Disagree   Agree   Strongly Agree

10. There are clear opportunities for me to work on appealing
    projects.

Strongly Disagree   Disagree   Agree   Strongly Agree

11. I have clear opportunities to advance (i.e. get promotions).

Strongly Disagree   Disagree   Agree   Strongly Agree

12. Robust training is available as I learn new tasks and roles.

Strongly Disagree   Disagree   Agree   Strongly Agree

13. There is a high level of psychological safety (feel safe even when conflicting opinions arise).

Strongly Disagree   Disagree   Agree   Strongly Agree

14. My company is objectively doing better than our competitors.

Strongly Disagree   Disagree   Agree   Strongly Agree

15. My company is always staying on pace with rising technologies.

Strongly Disagree   Disagree   Agree   Strongly Agree

16. My company has good processes to help adopt new technologies.

Strongly Disagree   Disagree   Agree   Strongly Agree

17. I have not looked for another job in at least six months.

Strongly Disagree   Disagree   Agree   Strongly Agree

18. The turnover rate here is quite low. (i.e. Most colleagues stick around for years.)

Strongly Disagree   Disagree   Agree   Strongly Agree

19. Mistakes are expected, and support exists to help us learn from them.

Strongly Disagree   Disagree   Agree   Strongly Agree

20. When others ask me where I work, I am proud to talk about my company.

Strongly Disagree   Disagree   Agree   Strongly Agree

Scoring: Add up every "Disagree," then every "Agree," and finally every "Strongly Agree" score. Plug the totals into the following equation to get the final score.

# of Disagree   _____ (Carry this same #) = _____
# of Agree   _____ (Multiply this by 2) = _____
# of Strongly Agree   _____ (Multiply this by 3) = _____

Add the numbers on the right. **Total** = _____ (out of 60)

If your score is 50 or higher, you agreed or strongly agreed with nearly everything. That's great! You are probably in a good place. Any job search in this instance should be purely to create a backup plan in case your company suffers a catastrophic or unexpected problem that causes layoffs or a company closure.

If your score is 30 to 49, it is worth pondering what issues you scored as "disagree" or "strongly disagree." Are they worth leaving for? Ask your mentor for guidance.

If your score is less than 30, you have indicated that you disagree or strongly disagree more often than you agree or strongly agree. In other words, you selected mostly negatives. You should reexamine your relationship with your current workplace and consider other options

Of particular interest, if you feel like your personal purpose in life is misaligned with the company's mission (question 1), or if you have one or more bullies/difficult personalities in your daily life (question 7), you deserve better. It would be best if you discussed alternatives with your mentor and trusted friends and family.

Survey: How Good is Your Supervisor?

You can rate your supervisor across various subjective measures in the following checklist. Take a moment beforehand to guess how positive your supervisor is from zero (the worst imaginable) to 48 (the best imaginable).

Initial Guess Score: _____

If your initial guess score is shockingly different from the total derived from scoring all the questions below, that is worth exploring. Circle a single answer per question.

1. My supervisor cares about me.

Strongly Disagree   Disagree   Agree   Strongly Agree

2. My supervisor aligns with positive company culture.

Strongly Disagree   Disagree   Agree   Strongly Agree

3. My supervisor focuses on my stated needs.

Strongly Disagree   Disagree   Agree   Strongly Agree

4. My supervisor recognizes the excellent work that I do.

Strongly Disagree   Disagree   Agree   Strongly Agree

5. My supervisor ensures I get the training to do great work.

Strongly Disagree   Disagree   Agree   Strongly Agree

6. My supervisor works with me on a development plan so I can grow toward my goals.

Strongly Disagree Disagree Agree Strongly Agree

7. My supervisor gives me grace whenever possible.

Strongly Disagree Disagree Agree Strongly Agree

8. My supervisor is available as much as I need them to be.

Strongly Disagree Disagree Agree Strongly Agree

9. My supervisor is effective at disrupting negative behaviors on the team.

Strongly Disagree Disagree Agree Strongly Agree

10. My supervisor is also a mentor to me.

Strongly Disagree Disagree Agree Strongly Agree

11. My supervisor will be at the company for a long time.

Strongly Disagree Disagree Agree Strongly Agree

12. My supervisor does not claim credit for the ideas of others.

Strongly Disagree   Disagree   Agree   Strongly Agree

13. There is a high level of psychological safety when speaking with my supervisor.

Strongly Disagree   Disagree   Agree   Strongly Agree

14. I believe my supervisor cares for my well-being, at least as much as my productivity.

Strongly Disagree   Disagree   Agree   Strongly Agree

15. My supervisor is interested in my advancement more than keeping me in my current role.

Strongly Disagree   Disagree   Agree   Strongly Agree

16. My supervisor gives me evaluations that make sense.

Strongly Disagree   Disagree   Agree   Strongly Agree

Scoring: Add up every "Disagree," then every "Agree," and finally every "Strongly Agree" score. Plug the totals into the following equation to get the total.

# of Disagree _____ (Carry this same #) = _____

# of Agree _____ (Multiply this by 2) = _____

# of Strongly Agree _____ (Multiply this by 3) = _____

Add the numbers on the right. **Total** =_____ (out of 48)

If your score is 40 or higher, you agreed or strongly agreed with nearly everything. That's great! Supervisors like this are quite helpful. Any searching you do for another should be solely to have a backup plan in case of catastrophic events you cannot foresee.

If your score is 24 to 39, it is worth pondering what issues you scored as "disagree" or "strongly disagree." Are they worth leaving for? Ask your mentor for guidance unless that mentor is your supervisor. Consider bringing significant issues to your supervisor if you feel the score to question 13 was "strongly agree."

If your score is less than 24, you disagreed or strongly disagreed more often than you agreed or strongly agreed. You should reexamine your relationship with this supervisor and consider other options. Other roles at your current company might be a good fit but understand that if you apply, your current supervisor will be alerted to that application.

You deserve a positive relationship with your supervisor, so consider your options if you don't. If you do, count your blessings.

CHAPTER 7
WHEN THINGS DON'T GO WELL

As you master your new knowledge about invisible forces at work and continue to grow your kindness practice, you will still encounter problems. You will make mistakes, and so will colleagues and supervisors. You might frustrate your colleagues by missing a key deliverable or clicking on an emailed link allowing hackers to hold your company's servers hostage. A colleague could take credit for your ideas, or your supervisor might overlook you during promotion time. Forces outside your control could make your life miserable, such as your company changing strategy, adjusting budgets, and engaging in layoffs. Your supervisor could suddenly get painfully quiet, leaving you wondering if you will still have a job the next day. Gossipers could spread unflattering rumors about you that rattle your supervisor's trust. When the next problem surfaces and you do nothing or possibly do the wrong thing, you could get locked in a perpetual whirlwind of fear and doubt, find yourself unemployed, or experience a situation that leaves you feeling deeply ashamed for years.

What can you do about the big problems when they arise? How can you tackle these issues in kind ways?

Since there are many varieties of obstacles to your health, happiness, and forward progress in the workplace, let's look at each different type in turn. Preparing ahead of time will give you an advantage when problems arise. Knowing what can block your path or generate awkward or difficult times allows you to plan your responses. Then, when actual problems arise, even though they may not be exactly what you expect, you will look like a pro as you handle them.

So, what can go wrong? A lot.

SCENARIO #1: YOU DO SOMETHING WRONG

While at work, you might worry about two kinds of missteps–getting something wrong in the work you were hired to do or getting something wrong with the other people involved. Making mistakes in the work itself is inevitable and should be anticipated by your trainers, teammates, and supervisor early on. Over time, these should still be expected, though at lower rates. However, mistakes involving messy interactions with the other humans you work with can keep you up at night. Let's unpack both issues and explore strategies for dealing with them.

Especially for newer employees, colleagues should expect mistakes related to unfamiliar processes. It is a lot like musicians who make more mistakes more often simply because they practice a lot. They get better not by avoiding picking up the instrument but by frequently picking it up and practicing. Not taking the proper steps in the proper order will make a deliverable go out late, leading to annoyed teammates and lost revenue. Depending on who makes a mistake, how early in their career they are, and how big the mistake is, most organizations will take these problems in stride most of the time. After all, most mistakes are related to a system, not to a single person's decision.

Think about it. If an employee carries out a task, but it is the wrong one, done wrong, or in the wrong order, a good work process should have quality checks in place, so the employee gets feedback early and often. If those alerts are not in place, the system needs improvement. Placing blame on a single well-intentioned colleague serves no one. Two distinct characteristics of an imperfect workplace, or one that is downright toxic, include individuals shouldering the burden of blame frequently and rarely revised work processes.

How can you prevent excessive work process errors? What do you do when you make them? The short answer is to keep your eyes and ears open. As you are taught how to work through a process, ask questions throughout and take notes. If there are Standard Operating Procedures (SOPs), read them. If there are work instructions, read them. When you are ready to work on a process, ask a seasoned employee to watch you do it or review your work. By working hard to learn the process correctly in the first place, you reduce the chances that you will perform the task incorrectly and decrease the potential for anyone doubting your earnestness.

The last thing to say about avoiding and correcting mistakes while doing your work involves common sense. If you think something is wrong, trust your instincts and speak up. If you see someone else doing the process differently, get curious and ask questions about their method so you can either learn a better way or help that colleague correct their mistakes. If your gut tells you to speak up about something, trust yourself and speak up; and when you do so, ask questions rather than pointing blame.

Unintentionally doing the wrong thing on the human side of work happens in the blink of an eye. I have called people the wrong name, given a hug when the recipient really wanted a smile, and walked into the wrong bathroom to a stunned audience who had no idea why I was there or what they should do. These moments of burning embarrassment can usually be handled with a quick apology and a note to yourself on how to do better next time. Still, sometimes the shame overwhelms and shuts down our ability to form words. An apology in the next day or two can heal these minor traumas.

What powerful emotions drive your bad behavior? Remember that you can analyze your limiting beliefs using an earlier chapter of this book, but the driving forces are often fear-based. In the heat of the moment, it can be easy to take action to undercut a rival, decry a peer who was promoted over you, or talk bad about the supervisor who decided not to take your advice. Where did that anger or frustration come from? Typically, you can find yourself afraid that you are not enough, that your actions are not enough, and that you are falling unrecoverably far behind where you should be. It is usually not about that peer or that supervisor. It is almost always about how you view and react to the situation.

If you overstep, offend, or otherwise harm someone in the office, make amends as soon as possible. The suffering person might need to hear you say you regret what happened and know how to avoid the same mistakes again. Accept the entire blame for your part in the situation and listen carefully to the reaction to validate the colleague's thoughts, feelings, and perspectives. Some recipients of apologies will want to hear you ask for forgiveness. If the situation is dire, offer to make up for the problem by taking actions they recommend as a form of restitution.

A crucial point about making mistakes and apologizing is to remember that if you have made an honest attempt to make up for the mistake, remember to forgive yourself. This essential step, if overlooked, can leave you anchored in place by the shame you bear. So, if you misgender someone, make a profoundly thoughtless comment to a colleague, or insult someone's culture, be brave by looking them in the eye while you admit the mistake and ask for forgiveness. No matter their reaction, you can feel like your attempts to restore trust and do the right thing should allow you this final step of self-forgiveness.

SCENARIO #2: A WELL-INTENTIONED COLLEAGUE
DOES SOMETHING WRONG

If a colleague makes a mistake that hurts your workflow—
or your feelings—remember a few critical pieces of information about that person. First, they are probably invested in
doing a great job and treating you well. Assuming positive intent is a helpful way of getting inside the other's thought processes, humanizing them, and remembering that, chances are,
they have no desire to be a villain. Second, your strong feelings
about the situation could overwhelm you and your colleague
if you let them burst out. It is good to take a moment to cool
down, get fresh air or a bite to eat, and think about how you
want to respond before actually responding. This cool-down
activity serves as self-care and relationship preservation, in
other words kindness to self and others all at once. When you
come together to discuss what went wrong, having that clearer
perspective and calmer emotions will make the interaction
smoother. This will allow you to give more grace than you
might otherwise.

When you interact with someone who got things wrong,
proper feedback delivery methods are helpful. Get curious
about what could have happened. Focus on how things could
unfold next time rather than dwelling too hard on the recent
issue. Any feedback you give is best done by describing how
you felt about the incident, what it was in unemotional and
precise ways, and stating the impact it has on you regarding

similar future situations. For example, "I felt demeaned and trivialized when you talked about cornbread as the cuisine of 'my people,' and it made me hope to avoid future small talk with you about food and culture." This feedback is clear, unemotional, accurate, and talks about the impacts on you, so it is likely to get the conversation started well.

Several key factors can be helpful in difficult conversations. Make sure you speak calmly, in low tones, and slowly so the conversation feels calm and measured. Be next to the person rather than across from them since this signals a desire to be close and face the issues together as a team rather than facing off like opponents.

As with any breakdown in a relationship, when new problems come at you, remember to stay curious. Ask questions, try to understand your colleague's goals, and see if anything you discover changes your perspective. In heated moments, I recommend the following phrases:

- "I appreciate your honest opinion."

- "Thank you for letting me know how you see this."

- "I don't see this the same way, but sharing your thoughts lets me know that my perspective is not the only one."

- "Let's agree to disagree."

- "Maybe we can table this discussion until later so we can move on with the primary goal?"

SCENARIO #3: A CONTENTIOUS COLLEAGUE DOES SOMETHING WRONG

Whether you ever understand the reasons or not, some colleagues are not interested in being friendly with you. If this is the pattern, you have a different set of considerations than with a friendly colleague. This latest interaction where things did not go well could be part of a larger pattern. Good behavior is essential no matter the circumstance, so insist on it. You deserve kind interactions, so it will never be okay for abrasive or abusive actions to come your way.

When a colleague says something derogatory like, "You are just an admin," it can feel so belittling that it feels unbelievable, even shocking, that someone would have thought to say it. To be clear, it is not okay for any colleague to make toxic, judgmental statements. Making that situation right can happen in several ways, but the first step is radical acceptance. Believing that someone would actually say or do something deliberately toxic is the starting point. Step two is to get curious and ask plainly, "When you say, 'You are just an admin,' what do you mean by that?" No matter what the answer is, you have demonstrated that you are not easily belittled, that you are curious, and that others' words and actions have consequences; the consequence being that the aggravator needs to think through and explain a condescending, unkind remark.

"You really messed this project up and now we are all screwed," stated in front of a meeting full of people is jarring and upsetting. Fearlessly stepping right into the statement, not with anger and yelling but instead with a focus on common goals is downright heroic in the moment. It is kind. The simple response of, "The issue at hand needs to be our focus. Blamestorming solves nothing, demotivates us all, and keeps us from focusing on the most important thing right now: fixing the issue." Again, this kind of response is kind to all involved, including the would-be blamestormer. In the analysis of how things went wrong in the first place, it is unlikely that a single person holds all the blame and, even if that were the case, then the approach to the work was flawed.

It is tricky handling hot, visceral moments such as the two examples above. It takes great maturity and practice to keep focusing on the common goals, on being curious, and redirecting the conversations to solutions. The end result, however, is that you look like a calm, practical, and kind partner. This makes you memorable for all the right reasons and leaves those who would lay judgment or accusations at your feet being remembered for very different reasons.

Ultimately, you do not have to trust the colleague in question, nor do you have to tolerate bad behavior that is consistent and/or extreme. Keep records of all interactions, even ones that get resolved to your satisfaction, so you can have details in case you ever want to push concerns to HR or a lawyer. Note that if it ever gets to that level, it is worth taking the "How Healthy is Your Workplace for You?" survey at the end of the previous chapter again because it is likely you have crossed over significant toxic workplace thresholds since you last took it.

Regardless of how things turn out between you and your colleague, remember to lead honestly and kindly. Even if what you get back is falsehoods and cruelty, at least you can feel good about sticking to your beliefs. Also, if things are not going well, you can determine exit strategies so nobody can take advantage of you.

SCENARIO #4: A LEADER CHANGES THINGS IN WAYS YOU DON'T LIKE

The main difference between leaders and your other colleagues is the power differential. When a leader makes a decision, you could think of it as a mistake or a problem, but it may not be either. It could simply be good corporate strategy that you don't particularly agree with or know enough about to have a truly informed opinion. Regardless of motivations and the actual decisions being made, these changes can feel large because they affect multiple aspects of the workplace, including your and your colleagues' daily lives. Leaders can trim the budget, taking away perks like free coffee and tea in the breakroom. Worse yet, they can reduce the company's contributions to your retirement plan or even lay you off.

Many leaders I have worked with across several industries have been terrific. Even terrific ones, however, will inevitably have missteps that affect you. If significant changes happen at your company over time, remember to take the "How Healthy is Your Workplace for You?" survey at the end of the previous chapter every six months or whenever a significant change makes you think of it. Do so, especially if a significant change to your workplace arises that leaves you feeling elated or despondent. As for the role your leaders take in these changes, much of it comes from them, so think of why these changes are being made from the perspectives of those making the decisions.

Ask yourself why a particular decision was made. It often has nothing to do with you, even if it feels like it is personal. Early in my career, I could talk myself into believing everything had deep personal meaning, like when my supervisor canceled a meeting with me unexpectedly. I worried that she no longer wanted to meet with me because of something I had done. It turned out that sudden mouth pain necessitated an urgent trip to the dentist. The important lesson here is to stay calm, do research wherever you can, and don't assume it is about you.

But, what if it *is* personal? What if a leader berates you during a large meeting? You have to weigh several factors to handle something like this well. First, consider whether the leader has acted like this with you or anyone else before. If their record is spotless and you have known them for a while, approaching them with curiosity (and insistence on kind treatment) is your best bet.

On the other hand, if this is part of a larger pattern of misbehavior, record details on a calendar so that you can have the information handy. You can still approach them with curiosity and try to have a conversation about what happened, but understand that a pattern of abusive, bullying behavior should be trusted for what it is: a sign that more will come your way.

When a leader creates a very personal or more general difficulty for you in the workplace, calculate how receptive that leader is to receiving feedback, how important it is to you to have them recognize your opinion, and decide if it is a battle you want to fight. The risks are obvious: challenging a leader on a policy they are uninterested in changing or on a mistake they made while interacting with you that they see as unimportant could lead to you getting labeled by this leader in negative ways. On the other hand, a leader who has a track record of accepting feedback and responding well to it might handle your input in uplifting ways.

One last important note about leaders: they hang out together. Much as you and your colleagues will chat about your lives and the joys and challenges of the workplace, leaders do the same. If leaders label you as helpful, technical, efficient, or a rising leader, other leaders will hear more about you. Similarly, if you are labeled as difficult or a complainer, that is equally likely to spread to other leaders at your company. So, if you raise a concern, it needs to be worth the risk.

A great strategy for getting your concerns across to a leader is to engage influencers, people the leader will listen to. If those influencers can raise concerns and get leaders to reconsider policies and decisions based on the merits of a data-backed argument, then you only have to engage those influencers in dialog about those concerns. You will not need to suggest that your ideas are the only right ones or that you disagree with something in particular. Just ask good questions and present data to back up your thoughts, then the influencers can take these thoughts to leadership where changes might happen.

SCENARIO #5: CULTURAL CLASHES CAUSE ISSUES

If your cultural background is different from colleagues around you, you can say or do the wrong thing and feel immediate shame and embarrassment. You could be from an ethnic group that's different from most of your colleagues, or you could be a different gender. Being born on foreign soil and moving to a new country means you bring a heritage that's naturally different from where you are working unless a lot of your compatriots somehow make up most of that company.

Friends of mine from Canada mentioned once that their ideas on how to connect with others and engage new acquaintances involves a lot more authentic vulnerability than what their new circle of friends are used to. The point is well-taken, however, whether the "clash" is between Americans and those who immigrated, or among different racial groups, gender preference groups, states in the U.S., or city versus country.

A dear colleague of mine said he once had a supervisor who compared the skin colors of people on the team and "deduced" that two of his teammates must surely be from similar "tribes." It is hard to calculate how much damage that supervisor did through this sort of thoughtless strategy of making guesses rather than listening and learning.

In my experience as someone with lots of privilege and advantages in my own country, one where we still struggle with racism, sexism, and other -isms, a lot of mindful learning is critical to relating to people from cultures you don't know well. It is all about genuine interest in learning about other cultures by attending a wide variety of cultural events, listening a lot, practicing what you know, and educating yourself.

Many companies have Employee Resource Groups (ERGs) that help give voice to various communities, including colleagues who are Black or African American, Latinx, LGBTQIA+, Asian, people with disabilities, and veterans. Female employees might also have an ERG, and so might remote employees. The benefit of these communities is that they are great support systems for employees who are core members of those groups plus the allies who want to stand with them. These communities help raise awareness of women's health, racial inequalities, and other critical topics. Further, they help celebrate big festivals and learning occasions, such as Diwali, Black History Month, Pride events, Hispanic Heritage Month, Hannukah, and Memorial Day.

My favorite part of learning about various groups of which I am not part is that I learn about the rich traditions, music, food, dances, and celebrations. By investing time in getting to know my colleagues, I make every aspect of my life richer. The happiness that comes with learning about and celebrating our differences is enormous. If the only culture I know is my own, I can only celebrate one set of events, but when I learn about five other cultures, life moves from black and white to full color. I suddenly have the potential for five times the number of foods, languages, dances, artwork, and celebrations compared with what I am used to. Better still, I have the potential for five times the number of friends I have had in the past.

If problems arise between you and a colleague whose culture is not your culture (perhaps their heritage, upbringing, or country of origin is not the same as yours), learn everything you can about their background so that you can better connect with them authentically. I once had an interaction with a leader who was born and raised in Russia while I was born and raised in the United States. I was in line to take up a leadership role under him, but as initial discussions gave way to follow-up conversations and emails, I found I was no longer aligned with him. I was suddenly out of consideration. I explored some of the reasons that could have gotten in the way, and one of them was simple: written summaries of our conversations made him worry. In Russian culture, repeating yourself can be seen as rehearsing a lie, so every time I wanted to summarize or clarify something I didn't understand, it set off alarm bells for this Russian colleague that I could never have guessed at. My scrappy, organizational focus came across as me not paying enough attention in the first place, as arguing with decisions that were already made, or even worse, as rehearsing deceptions. Had I known more about this leader, either through conversations with other leaders I already knew or through reading more about Russian culture, I could have avoided these misperceptions.

To avoid similar issues, do your research on cultural conflicts that you can see coming. Sometimes, quietly listening and learning from another person from another religious or ethnic background, or who was born in another country, gives you the best information on what is valued, desired, and necessary for a good working relationship. Please don't try to guess. Instead, pay attention during ice breakers and introductions at meetings to learn more about each colleague in their own words. Some colleagues are on the Internet, perhaps giving lectures on YouTube, presenting their background on LinkedIn, or otherwise making themselves known by articles. Invest time in getting to know as much as you can about them.

If you ever find you and a colleague are "talking past" each other, ask yourself if the problem could be unspoken cultural differences. If that colleague suspects you cannot understand their cultural perspective so they cannot speak their full truth, this stifles authentic connection. Use the suggestions above about doing research, listening well during ice breakers and introductions, and genuinely celebrating other cultures. When others see you as curious and caring, the odds are in your favor of making new and lasting friendships.

SCENARIO #6: YOUR COMPANY CULTURE AND/OR STRATEGIES SHIFT

A tricky part of working is knowing your company can evolve. You are embedded within the culture, working on projects, and doing daily tasks, so changes can feel glacial, even imperceptible. Some changes can be quick, like when you're asked to move cross-country to a new site that seems so different compared to the one you're used to. To the newly hired at that new site, however, they feel like how things are when they first show up is "how things have always been."

Regardless of how big or small the changes are or how comfortable you are with them, there are strategies for handling them well. Your first and most important strategy is radical acceptance–admit that the changes are actually taking place. The most common barrier to taking action in difficult situations is disbelief that things are suddenly unfolding around you in the ways that they are. So, accept reality and even say it out loud if needed, "This is real. I have to deal with this."

A series of questions and the research you do to answer them can help illuminate your stance on a given change. The first question is one of ethics. Are those affected given enough time to adapt to the change, or was it abrupt? Are current colleagues being treated fairly and kindly during the change?

If you are okay with the ethical implications of the change, the next question is how you align philosophically. A company changing its mission from selling fast food to selling healthier foods might fit beautifully with your desire to supply people with foods that make them live longer and feel better. On the other hand, you may have loved the foods your company offered and be saddened by abandoning the products that drew you to the company in the first place. The last big question to consider involves how you can live in harmony with the change. Will you need extra training? Are you well-positioned and ready to help others? If your experience and education are just right, you could ride the waves of change into higher positions of authority.

When changes come to your company, different colleagues will have different reactions along a spectrum. Those who love challenges and learning new things will latch onto the change, learn all about it, and thrive. Others who cannot stand the idea of changes might retire or seek other employment. Most others will be somewhere in the middle—perhaps complaining a bit but adapting minimally as needed, or maybe learning what they can as time permits with excitement and energy. Ask yourself where you want to be: hiding and hoping the change isn't too big or helping lead the charge on how to make the big changes work well? When you see change as something that shakes opportunities loose for you, you can demonstrate your skills and energy and thrive within your shifting corporate landscape.

SCENARIO #7: A COLLEAGUE NEEDS YOUR HELP

Everyone needs a helping hand sometimes. When it is your turn, you hope you have a colleague nearby who sees you getting knocked down and helps you get back on your feet. With your superpower of kindness, you are well-equipped to be that same supportive colleague for them when and if the time comes.

To be a great ally to anyone at work, regardless of who they are and what kind of help they need, listen and believe them. Ask how you can help. Stand up for them.

I love having colleagues I can learn from. The more different from me they seem on the surface, the deeper I am willing to dig to find delight in that relationship as a result. The payoff is tremendous if I can listen through discomfort, truly hear them, and become a friend.

What if there are few colleagues different from you? If the workplace is not diverse, consider asking your supervisor and even your leadership why. Without the push from "average" employees for more diversity at work, you will never know the richness of having those colleagues around you. Discover the demographics of who works at your company and encourage more diversity on interviewing panels. Push for hiring that involves a diverse slate of candidates for every role. Qualified and brilliant people of all kinds exist and sometimes locating those candidates involves word-of-mouth, personally asking people to apply, or having recruitment show up at career fair events with diverse candidates.

When new colleagues join your team, invest your time and effort in team-building activities. As colleagues allow themselves to be vulnerable, you can learn more about them, so encourage others to share what they feel comfortable with. Reach out to new colleagues and include them in lunch plans. Ask how colleagues can feel supported, and make efforts to support them in those ways. When your kindness guides your actions, you will be the warm, welcoming, supportive colleague everyone wants as a friend.

SCENARIO #8: LIFE HAPPENS

In early 2023, while I was writing this book, I put a snack down at the kitchen table and felt my eyes cross. I sat down, blinked my eyes a few times to find it wouldn't go away. When I called my wife to the room, she asked me a few questions only to find I was slurring the few words I could still form. With two of my kids propping me up, I watched from the inside as big functions of my brain shut down.

I was having a stroke.

The ambulance delivered me to the hospital, and overnight a team of healthcare professionals brought me back from being unable to walk, speak, and think clearly to "normal." At my hospital bed, my doctor asked how I was doing. I insisted that I ate well and was active, but he responded that it was not enough. He suggested I think hard about factors that could have triggered my stroke, especially unpredictable nutrition, lack of sleep, and stress.

I was guilty on all charges.

Despite writing a book about kindness, one that talks about kindness to oneself, I neglected self-care. On top of my busy day job and writing a book, I had frequent difficult relationship conversations with my wife. We were raising two teens and supporting our 20-year-old who lived nearby. Our contractor was building an addition to our house for my mother-in-law. Added to that, we had a cat who interrupted our sleep every night, leaving me with four hours of sleep most nights.

In short, I took for granted that my healthy body would tolerate anything, but I finally took on too many burdens. My body had had enough. I was sure that my health would stay tough and strong no matter what I asked of myself. I was completely wrong.

In addition to meds, I have amended my ways. The threat of losing brain function is a tremendous motivator. While I cannot eliminate stress or dictate perfectly how my sleep and nutrition will be, I can pursue strategies involving meditation, regular exercise, blocking time for sleep, and keeping healthy snacks with me.

In your life, I sincerely hope you avoid moments and seasons of poor health. I hope you do everything that makes sense for your situation to promote great health for a long and happy life. Keep that kindness compass firmly in hand and remember to use it unsparingly on yourself. Engage in good, regular self-care and renew not only your health but also your perspective.

Beyond unexpected left turns in your life, plenty of other things can happen to make it hard to focus on work. Perhaps the health of a beloved family member or friend deteriorates. Maybe it is a disaster at your home or in your town. The exact nature of the emergency is less important than what you do about it. Regardless of the other events swirling around you, make time for yourself each day. Meditate, practice yoga or tai chi, select nourishing meals, stay hydrated, and make time for good sleep. Whatever the keys are to your physical and mental health, do those things. Let your supervisor know as much of your situation as you feel comfortable revealing, enough so they can lend support but perhaps not so much that they worry about giving you important projects in the short or long term. Surrounding yourself with the right support system will allow you to connect more with those who help you. It will also allow you to recharge enough so that your kindness superpower will be available as much as you need it to help others you care about. Then, check in on your colleagues, friends, and family. People remember when other people reach out. That kindness compass leading you to support others shows, at a bare minimum, how much you care.

CLOSING

My friend, Kipp Spanbauer, has a great saying whenever I'm feeling like problems have gotten too big or if it seems like I will never have problems again because things are so great: "Things are never as good as you hope or as bad as you fear." That is his way of telling me to slow down, calm myself, and prepare for a realistic outcome rather than one that involves rainbows and kittens, or star systems being blown apart by Darth Vader.

Problems will arise. When they do, huge emotions can arise as well. The advice in this chapter should help you navigate all sorts of difficulties, confusion, and problems and see the positive sides when challenges arise. Take slow deep breaths, trust your kindness practice, and give yourself time to work through whatever has you worried. You don't have to solve everything in one sitting or at one meeting, so patiently weigh alternatives, consult with mentors and trusted colleagues, and follow the path of greatest kindness and greatest integrity.

The tools and takeaways below give you a thorough process for approaching problems and issues that arise in the workplace.

TOOLS AND TAKEAWAYS

When workplace difficulties arise that feel confounding, like trying to find a handhold on a difficult rock climb, there are some general strategies for how to handle them outlined below. Each of these six steps is essential when dealing with difficult situations in healthy, positive, and kind ways. You may not need to delve deeply into every step, but every step should get full consideration.

The six steps in responding to a difficult situation are: prepare, self-care, address the moment, educate, hold people accountable, and move forward.

Prepare

Constant learning is a big part of preparing for difficult situations, whether they arise from your actions, those of a colleague or leader at your company, or something more abstract such as industry forces. Just by picking up this book and delving into all the concepts up to this point, you have already prepared yourself for many situations that might come your way. Keep reading books, articles, and business reports about your industry. Take courses, earn certifications, and consider earning a degree related to your work or work you wish you could be doing. The more you know, the more prepared you are for handling problems that present themselves. Learning should never stop.

When it comes to colleagues or customers, understand that the vast majority of people are easy to work with as long as their needs, spoken or unspoken, are met. Those who see you as an ally will generally treat you well but occasionally misstep. The best way to prepare yourself for difficult interactions with well-meaning colleagues is to have a robust kindness practice. Create a regular morning calendar entry in which you engage in practices and exercises already recommended in this book and practice consistently.

Treating colleagues as kindly as you know how to means that your reputation is likely to precede you. This will help you cultivate a network of allies, close colleagues, and friends within your work culture who will have your back in hard situations. Your maturing kindness practice lays the groundwork of good habits, like leading with kindness and assuming positive intent on the part of others even when communications get muddled or become negative. When significant interactions go poorly, you may already have rapport and mutual respect. It is powerful to have a general well-meaning and kind impression of one another.

Unfortunately, some colleagues and customers will choose bad behavior. Full stop. If you can delve into motivations for why they choose self-serving behaviors, it could be worthwhile; however, getting new behaviors to blossom within some colleagues only happens if they are motivated to learn these better behaviors. That motivation largely comes from within; thus, helping a colleague eager to make a change will be much more worthwhile than expending energy to convince a colleague with little or no motivation to change. Knowing the difference between those who consistently choose unkind behaviors from those who hope for kind interactions is critical.

A last word on preparing—know who your crew and mentors are, and make your kindness practice robust. Nurturing your network and reaching out to your mentors needs to be a regular practice. Those allies will help ground you before the good and bad happen in the workplace.

Self-care

Take care of your basic needs. Get sleep, stay hydrated, eat well, exercise, connect with friends and family, and pursue hobbies you enjoy. This sounds so basic, but during stressful times these can be easy to neglect as if they are unimportant. They are very important, so pay special attention to them!

Write down new gratitudes daily so you can remember that there are positive things in the world. Doing this primes you to be more creative, better at problem-solving, and generally happier. All of this contributes to you handling difficult interactions with a greater sense of possibility which almost always leads to better outcomes.

Address the Moment (depending on what kind of moment it is)

When a problem arises, breathe slowly and calmly to keep your approach anchored in reason and logic. Any big emotions that arise are worthy of addressing, eventually. If emotions grow so intense that you become reactive, you could make matters worse.

Establish the facts as clearly and objectively as possible. Until you know for certain from the primary sources involved, you could be working with incomplete or incorrect information. Understanding the genuine, detailed nature of the issue is more important than having an impressive reaction time.

Engage those who have solved similar problems. If you

think that engaging some colleagues too early could cause more problems, get the advice of your mentors. You may not need to do anything, so getting this advice first can be critical. Remember that not every problem is yours to solve, so getting this advice can keep you from stepping into a situation that could be to your detriment.

If the problem you encounter is people-based, meaning that someone has behaved in ways counter to the established work culture, a multitude of factors could be in play. Be sure to discuss the problem when all parties are calm and in a setting where there is the least possibility of embarrassment and shame.

Use your kindness compass. By employing your superpower of kindness, thinking of, and implementing the kindest action you can for everyone involved, you live out your values and maximize the odds of a good outcome. Even if good outcomes do not arise, at least you can feel good about the actions you took.

When negativity strikes, make sure that your closest allies know your preference for assuming positive intent. By making sure your work crew avoids unkind responses on your behalf and instead engages in responses that you would engage in, difficult relationships will not get worse when you are absent. Instead, colleagues who have conflict with you will get the impression that your entire circle of friends engages in assuming positive intent, being curious, and acting kindly. It is not just you, but your entire work crew who will value alignment, deeper understanding, and kindness.

Beyond your colleagues, leaders at your company will learn of your reputation for being kind. When things go wrong, they will be more likely to seek out your input before casting judgment. Few things are more powerful than having a leader who is ready to defend you because they know your basic approach to working well with others. That said, carefully consider engaging leaders in difficulties and have some solutions at the ready when you do. Unless you are the decision-maker related to the problems at hand, propose your solutions as options, never as a an already adopted direction, and then listen to the decision maker's counsel.

Educate

When things don't go well with a colleague, it is a great opportunity to learn and teach. Perhaps that colleague is oblivious. Sometimes people are tired, distracted, or they might simply have limited emotional intelligence. Possibly, the colleague has little experience with the situation at hand, with the ethnic cultures involved, and the list goes on.

Seeing this difference between you and your colleague is the beginning of being able to teach and help them do better. If they say something inappropriate, let them know clearly, "That feels hurtful and unkind." It can be invaluable to provide careful, objective feedback, such as describing the situation in unemotional terms or giving feedback in terms of how you personally felt without embellishment.

Being curious about why the colleague acted in the ways that they did can hasten your own learning. Ask questions and suspend judgment since it could be a cultural difference, a case of someone mishearing someone else, or other issues that don't make sense until you have all the answers. It is also possible that your colleague has limiting beliefs that they have never explored, so ask questions or even recommend sections of this book.

Hold Others Accountable

Sometimes things go wrong, and nobody is to blame. Other times, someone is to blame for a problem, but there is no way to hold them to account. But, what if a colleague caused harm and made no attempt to fix the problem?

In a healthy workplace, bad behavior will have repercussions. Your supervisor, other leaders at your company, and Human Resources (HR) partners should take care of issues that arise as long as they are aware. If you must be the one to make them aware, remember that you do not have to face the situation alone. Reach out to your mentors and trusted members of your network for any support you need. Make sure you have accurate and extensive records and share those with the officials at your company who need to know about them, whether that's your supervisor, HR, an ethics hotline or department of ethics at your company, and your supervisor.

If things have gotten to a legal level, such as being the recipient of sexual harassment or racially discriminatory behavior, or any number of other illegal behaviors, engaging your Human Resources group at your workplace could be helpful. Once you engage them, however, you will probably find that you lose a lot of control over how the situation plays out after that.

Move Forward

Quite often, problems get resolved well. Good communications, positive intent, well-designed systems, and good leadership can add up to making the workplace a great one in which problems get fixed to the liking of most who were involved. The logical and easy next thing is to move forward.

When problems are not resolved to your liking, however, it can be easy to ruminate. If a problem was never resolved at all, or if it carries emotional weight, it can be hard to leave it alone. It can sting when leaders reach a conclusion that you disagree with.

In the case where you need to continue working with a colleague you don't particularly like because they engage in behaviors you don't care for, consider lowering your expectations for that colleague. There is no need to gossip about them. Instead, manage your expectations so that the next time you work with them you expect it just won't be as pleasant as it is with colleagues you prefer working with. By seeing this situation as it really is, you can be more matter-of-fact about the situation and make it through in a good mood.

In some cases, the only reasonable actions left are to make peace with the situation, leave it behind, and move on. Regardless of how a problem was resolved, you still have positive ways of moving forward using your own approach to work. Keep focused on your values, beliefs, and strategies. Polish your kindness practice. Strengthen your network. Connect more with your work friends, close colleagues, mentors, and other trusted individuals.

When things don't go right, you gain helpful information that increases your wisdom and experience. Someday, you may be in a position to help others avoid pitfalls, and believe me, you'll be grateful for all of these experiences then. Whatever you learn from more recent problems, model good behavior, and become a guiding light for others who may or may not know you, but who can then choose to respond in a kind and respectable manner because you were courageous enough to model how it is done.

CHAPTER 8
WE ARE STRONGER TOGETHER

In January 2018, a massive snowstorm hit the Eastern seaboard, covering my North Carolina home in a foot of snow. When heavy snow falls in this part of the country, there are not enough salt trucks and plows to clear the roads. School was cancelled for the kids, but thankfully we were spared the loss of electricity that sometimes comes with these big storms. With the kids still sleeping, my wife and I walked through our winter wonderland.

When I started work a bit later than usual, I noticed that Derek Campbell and some other teammates were not online. On a snow day, I expected nothing different; parents in the path of the blizzard would be situating their kids for a fun day playing in the snow or focused on arts and crafts or perhaps on iPads. By about midday, Derek had yet to log in or email to let me know he would be out to care for his kids. As I noticed this, Brian Pickett, his childhood friend who also worked on our team, sent me a message asking if he could call.

"Michael, I don't think there's any easy way to say this," I swallowed hard at Brian's words, "but Derek died in his sleep last night." I croaked, "What?" only to hear Brian confirm it. "Derek's gone."

Derek was in his mid-40s and in decent health. It seemed impossible that he could have died. Later, it was determined that a congenital heart defect stole Derek from us. There was no notice. It left his family in grief and his friends and work-mates sad, stunned, and disbelieving.

As the team leader, I had to act as the point person, coordi-nating how and when to tell everyone, providing information about counseling resources, and helping a mutual friend of Derek's and mine who had joined the team a week earlier. Our team and others we worked with needed to know we would be less efficient and raw with grief. Everyone needed kindness, and our superpower would be quickly depleted no matter what we did. Self-care and care for Derek's family had become most important to us as we navigated losing our friend.

In the long history of the human story, everyone currently here owes a debt to those who came before. As we find our way, others help us. None of us gets where we eventually end up without at least one person taking a chance on us. With Derek, he had taken chances to help nonstandard candidates join his old company, paving the way for my success and plen-ty of others. When it was time for him to join my team, know-ing I would have a former boss as a new direct report, I had to take a chance that our egos could get out of the way and allow us to work well together. I only made it where I was going because Derek Campbell gave me chances.

Over my career, I have had mentors and coaches like Dorothy Findlen, Jim Horn, Karen Adamson, Melissa Morrison, Kipp Spanbauer, Blake Doherty, and Kristen Hadeed. Their investment of time, patience, curiosity, and care is something I remember to honor by paying it forward to others whenever I get the chance. Some uplift in my life has been hard-fought and earned through blood, sweat, and tears. So much more—vastly more—has been gifted to me by kind souls who had long to-do lists, but still happily and warmly made time for me.

Who are the mentors, coaches, and risk-takers who helped pave your path? At least as important a question: How are you paying that kindness forward?

The odds are that you have had parents, aunts and uncles, teachers, and others who went above and beyond what they had to do. They saw something in you that made them challenge you hard, ask the right questions, have back-room conversations on your behalf, and otherwise open doors for you because they wanted to see you succeed.

Why do they do this? Why do we hunger to do this for each other?

I have been asked if our most base nature is to claw past each other on a quest to get the things we want, even if it means harming others to get there, or if it is to practice kindness and help support others to get things they want. To a large extent, helping others is where we get our most profound satisfaction and joy. Still, I have thought a lot about the question of our base nature. However, I think the question's premise is flawed. It encapsulates an either/or proposition that makes no sense.

Why does it have to be either/or? So many resources are available at any healthy company; you and a rival can both get what you need. Clawing past each other to get what you want makes you both look petty, slows you down, and makes it hard to accomplish your goals with all that friction you cause each other. Anyone else who isn't playing that game, who focuses on making good things happen for the company and everyone around them, is likely to launch right past anyone who sees only the game. Getting stuck in this mode where you worry incessantly about scarcity—a lack of resources, available upward paths, capital to spend, or time to complete tasks— means you miss the abundance apparent in your company's quarterly earnings reports. If your company frequently turns a profit, there is leeway for leaders to put support behind any project and any employee they want to prioritize.

When you work long and hard, hoping for a promotion while you do good work, it means approaching projects comprehensively, genuinely helping teammates, and delivering high-quality deliverables. What does it hurt for a rival who perhaps did less work or was less congenial while doing it to get a promotion simultaneously? Burrowing down into righteous indignation—that sense that you are more deserving, and some injustice has been done—doesn't help anyone. The objection to someone else's good fortune stems from the less noble side of your emotional landscape, the part far away from your kindness practice.

Why be upset with another, even a rival, who makes excellent gains? When looking back over the path you traveled to get to where you are, you run the risk of assuming someone else's path was shorter, or less painful., It can be easy to get stuck on the unfairness. It can feel dangerous that a rival has the power to skip steps and climb an easier path. You worry that their rate of advancement will land them a spot as your supervisor even though you might know more or have more profound experience. Worse, you worry that all your effort is meaningless.

Ask yourself: Was it meaningless to support teammates and company goals? Was it unimportant completing projects, improving processes, and bringing joy to those around me?

Of course, your efforts were meaningful. If aligned with your life's purpose, the company you work for is advancing an agenda that helps build the future you want to live in. The more you help, the more you live in your truth and the more real that future becomes, day by day. That is all priceless. Only ego, the drive to see yourself as either master of the Universe or the unfairly oppressed and misunderstood, could convince you that your efforts have little meaning.

What you don't know—what none of us knows—is the future. You don't own a magic crystal ball that gives 100% accurate answers. The guess that another's advancement is unfair or could mean bad things for you is not based on foreknowledge, but fear. It is based on ignoring your game by focusing too hard on someone else's.

Imagine that your rival's skillset (or progress or status) is a line segment. Maybe it is longer than yours, or maybe it is the same size. Looking at theirs next to yours, how do you shorten their line so you can have better chances? Ponder it. Can you cut theirs in half? That hardly seems fair, and it would likely mean doing something underhanded and sneaky to make it shorter, right?

The answer is shockingly simple: stop focusing on their line and make yours longer. If you get stuck thinking of their line, you give your power away. Why focus on something you cannot and should not control? That would mean diverting your attention from what others are doing to focus on another's game. Avoid doing that. Focus on making your game as strong as it can be. That is what you can control. That is where your energy can be constructively spent. Focus on that!

Back to the question of our nature: Are we self-serving creatures or those who can be generous? It all comes down to habit. If you are used to finding ways of helping others, injecting joy into their days (and yours as well as a brilliant side-effect), then that is the habit you will continue to reach for and build. Allowing yourself to act out of fear, to think of scarcity as you make sure to get "what's in it for me," will make you feel less generous, and a lot sadder over time. When compared so clearly, it becomes apparent what a powerful investment your robust kindness practice can be. This is not just for you, but also for those whose lives you touch.

Remember the concept of *ubuntu*—experiencing your humanity through the humanity of others. If that rival of yours has something to celebrate, imagine how they feel, how their family benefits from their advancement, and then celebrate with them. Give them your congratulations. If your only focus is on how they deserve or don't deserve what they get, it becomes difficult to practice kindness. Admittedly, with some colleagues at work, it is much easier to feel celebratory, but with practice, you can widen that circle and celebrate more colleagues authentically.

Earlier in the book, I made a big deal of choosing the people you affiliate yourself with, advising that you select your closest friends and colleagues wisely. While this advice still holds, I suggest you get outside of your close circle regularly and see how others do what they do. By regularly challenging your perspective, you remind yourself that yours is not the only perspective and you ensure your own growth.

While some perspectives will be startling, exciting, and worth exploring, sometimes you will simply disagree with the perspectives presented to you. For example, during parent's weekend at UNC, I have loved giving a planetarium show at Morehead Planetarium on the north side of campus. As a parent now and having graduated from UNC many years back, I could relate to the parents in the room not just as a cosmic tour guide, and not just as another parent, but also as someone who could relate to their kids' experiences of becoming a student at UNC.

The planetarium show went as planned. I showed everyone Orion the Hunter, the Big Dipper, the visible planets, and
the Moon. Squeezing in light, funny bits about each celestial
body as I described it, I heard the usual tittering where I expected, a guffaw and a snort at the really good joke about Ura-
nus, and finished the evening flying the audience out into
space to show them our solar system.

As parents filed out past my control console, many smiled
and thanked me. In any audience, I take it as a point of pride if
multiple people repeat something back to me, like "follow the
arc to Arcturus, take a hike-a to Spica...I will never forget that.
That's so good." The compliments started flowing in exactly
that way.

Then, a small, bearded man came up and drew me to the
side, away from the other parents. He said, "With all of this
amazing technical equipment, this wonderful capability that
you have right in front of you, and you gave us this garbage?
Infantile jokes? Silly talk?" His anger was palpable and stood
in stark contrast to the other reviews that were still coming in
from the other side of the control console.

Fortunately, I already knew the best way to handle this situation. I could tell that his emotional state had nothing to do
with me, so I thanked him for his willingness to share his perspective. I did not say or imply that I agreed with it, I simply
thanked him for sharing his thoughts. He threw a few angry
words at me about my response, and I said, "No, I'm really
grateful you shared your perspective with me." After he

stormed off, exasperated that I had given him absolutely nothing to push against, I never heard from him again. To this day, this is still the only bad review I have ever heard from any audience member, and I remain confident that my show presentation strategies satisfy most attendees. I absolutely reconsidered and rethought my strategies because of this comment, but in the end, there was nothing to change because the comments were internal ones that leaked out of that poor man.

When I travel across North America and various parts of Europe, South America, and Africa, I invariably pick up on nuances that don't usually spring to mind. Whenever I travel to countries where English is not the primary language, I gain a tremendous appreciation for anyone kind enough to try to help me in English. It reminds me that I have multiple colleagues back home who work very hard to speak with me in English, even though it must be challenging for them to speak and write for multiple hours per day in their non-native language.

Just commuting between a city and countryside on a daily commute can bring you from one set of political yard signs to another. These can remind you that the hard-working people in one area won't necessarily align, at least on the surface, with others who live just down the road. Digging a bit past those obvious misalignments, at the root of any voter's thought processes, are a sense of fairness, helping family and community, getting what is needed to survive, and handing out respect and kindness to those around you. In the shuffle of an election year, so much of that is forgotten. Suppose a rural citizen looks disdainfully at the yard signs in cities and vice versa. In that case, we can forget about assuming positive intent and lose sight of commonalities that span all communities.

The colleagues who show up to work with you each day can have very different origins than yours. While that could mean country versus city, it could also mean their political preferences, religion, gender preferences, gender identity, country of origin, native languages spoken, racial profile, introvert versus extrovert, and parent versus nonparent. By learning the similarities, such as the choice of where to work, you will realize how deeply connected you are. By getting to know the differences, you add spice, energy, and newness to your life in ways you couldn't possibly do on your own. In both cases, you bond with others, broaden your network, and learn different ways the world can work. As you learn more about those around you, you become less alone.

When I traveled to Addis Ababa, Ethiopia in early 2023, I expected to find a cornucopia of delicious differences from what I was accustomed to in Chapel Hill, North Carolina in the United States. I expected that language, food, music, travel, and demographics would be brilliantly different. I wondered if I would be seen as an intruder or a guest, as a worthwhile conversation partner or a nuisance.

What I found was more amazing and brilliant than I expected. As a white man in this beautiful African country, I quickly surmised that I was part of the minority. It certainly stirred up curiosity among the local schoolboys when I visited the city of Lalibela, Ethiopia, with my friends. As we walked along, the boys wanted to practice English with me and hoped I might give them money so they could go to the local street vendors. As my dear friend Bineyam handed them money, they laughed together as they promised to buy pencils and school supplies. Bineyam filled me in; what they'd said was code for candy and sweets. We laughed, recalling our own childhood experiences.

As I went to see the ancient, hand-carved stone churches that Lalibela is famous for, our tour guide connected with us repeatedly. His agreement was for a three-hour tour, but he contacted us ahead of our flight, met us at the airport with the hotel pick-up service, and checked in with us early each day and before bedtime each night. After the extensive two-part tour that took most of a day, he accompanied us to the airport and then phoned Bineyam a few hours later to make sure we had made it safely back to Addis Ababa.

This level of care and kindness flooded daily life in Ethiopia while I visited. Of course, Bineyam and Eyerusalem were accommodating at every turn, just like your dearest friends might be when you visit them in their birthplace for the first and, possibly, only time. Beyond the two of them, however, it was every cab driver, every waiter, and every friend and family member of Bineyam's and Eyerusalem's who welcomed me into their home. Whoever attended to me at mealtimes brought strong coffee in small cups with billows of smoke emanating from charred wood in wrought iron. The strange and interesting foods, full of flavor, sometimes with sweetness or spice, came to me on spread *injura*—a thin tangy, pancake-like bread—with several more rolls of *injura* available so I would never have a chance of going hungry.

As we traveled by car, each rotary (or "roundabout") had everything from foot traffic to mules or goats being led through by their owners amidst all kinds of vehicles. In the United States, during my daily commute, I regularly get the sense that the slightest annoyance can upset drivers who angrily flip you the bird. In Ethiopia, a completely different sense pervaded—one of everyone trying to make sure they got where they were going without causing anyone else any harm. As a motorcycle, cab, bus, or three-wheeled *bajaj* driver approached the rotary, he did so with earnest interest that a healthy outcome for all pedestrians, human or otherwise, was assured.

It would be easy to take up several pages with how amazing my trip to Ethiopia was, but the bigger point is simple: whether any event or situation felt foreign to my American sensibilities it was the kind human connections that dispelled potential fears before I even felt them and made each moment one I'll cherish for the rest of my life.

So please invite all kinds of colleagues from various backgrounds to share with you. Sharing during work hours is quick and easy. You just have to be brave and suggest it, or if you are the one in charge, make it happen.

A couple of years after Derek Campbell passed away, I started a new effort on my team at Gilead Sciences, the one that Derek, Bineyam, Kipp, and so many others have been a part of: I started each new team meeting with gratitudes. Our bonds to each other had already been strengthened through the process of grieving and recovering from the loss of Derek, but it sounded like a practice that would strengthen those bonds even more.

As a fully remote team of a dozen programmers, starting meetings with stating what we were each grateful for was a way to do several things simultaneously. First, I wanted to make sure that everyone felt comfortable speaking up during meetings. Having everyone speak for one minute right at the start of the meeting makes them feel comfortable. People who feel warmly welcomed and encouraged to share are more likely to speak up later when speaking about process innovations. Second, priming everyone to think about the joy in their lives helps them see that positive outcomes are possible. No, not just possible, but swimming in joyful moments worthy of celebration. When you think like that, it is okay to dare to look for positive options in work decisions as well. Third, it humanizes us to each other and builds trust when we talk about our gardens, anniversaries, pets, and family gatherings.

The unexpected nature of what each person chooses to share is where you get those tastes, how different each of us lives, and how beautiful those lives can be. To build the future we want to live in, everyone's voice must be heard so that the best of all cultures can merge together in harmony. It makes us all stronger for paying attention to differences we actively sought to learn rather than declaring that our way is the right way.

The concept of cherishing and honoring our differences is succinctly summarized in the *Star Trek* television series and movies: Infinite Diversity in Infinite Combinations, or IDIC. Out of all the science fiction series I have explored, the future world of *Star Trek* seems the most hopeful, equitable, and kind. The future depicted is the future I want to build and live in, and all of it starts with kindness.

TOOLS AND TAKEAWAYS

As you enter a workplace where you see a lot of differences in background, education, experience, or perspectives compared with what you are used to, learn everything you can. Absorb the joy that comes with learning about these exciting differences. You may not agree with everything that you hear or experience, but the odds are that it will feed your work practices and your life experiences in ways that will enhance your worldview.

At work, engage in celebrations put together by the company and by your colleagues that allow you to learn and grow. Engage with how your company gives back to the community, either through charitable giving or through volunteerism. As you get familiar with colleagues from various backgrounds, listen for ways that you can learn more and be supportive of various groups. If those ways involve reading, watching documentaries, or simply attending events with your colleagues outside of work, your life will be richer with each new action you take.

Bring Others Close to You

Creating mindful practices is a big part of tightening your network. Regardless of what race, ethnicity, gender, gender preference, disability status, or location you have compared with your workmates, there will be some colleagues who feel more distant than others. Here are four ways of bringing them closer.

1. Reach Out Regularly

Especially in a world that is hybrid, where colleagues might work from home, from the office, or a bit of each, it pays to have regular meetings. Even if you don't have a standing meeting with someone, mark it on your calendar to reach out to key colleagues at a frequency that makes sense. Calling, messaging, or having a video meeting allows you to recall topics during your interactions that might otherwise go unstated.

Anyone who is working remotely from a home office or who just doesn't overlap with you much in the office will truly appreciate the personal touch of hearing from you regularly, even if you don't have specific business to work out. List colleagues you feel you don't interact with enough or that you would like to know better. Add the high priority colleagues to your calendar, specifically inviting them to regular meetings or set up reminders to ensure you reach out. If there is an agenda, let them know that it is a chance to work through specific work items. If you just want a regular checkpoint, let them know that too. Done consistently over time, this practice will tighten your network. You'll be seen as a proactive leader who values relationships.

2. Support Others

If you have colleagues you perceive as different from you, especially if they are in a group that is regularly overlooked or mistreated where you may have more privilege, remember that they may have obstacles to overcome that feel unfamiliar to you. You will not know what those obstacles are, so express your interest in learning. Ask questions and aim to be a good ally. Ask what preferred support from you would look like, and then seek out opportunities to provide that support.

In the absence of any specific requests, maybe you could volunteer your time to a relevant cause or show up to ERG meetings and events. Perhaps your colleague wants to you to call attention to what they say when they do speak up but are ignored. This last item could be as simple as stating, "Hey, Julie just mentioned a great idea that I think we missed. Julie, can you say that idea again and elaborate?" By being visible and speaking up, we can help shine the spotlight on colleagues and let them know they matter.

3. Stay Curious

Your superpower of kindness is best fed by three factors: self-care, self-awareness, and curiosity. When thinking of others, curiosity is the element you need to feed. When a colleague acts in unexpected ways, ask questions, and try to understand their perspectives. When that colleague approaches issues in unfamiliar ways, ask questions. Regardless of anything going on in the world of your colleagues, trying better to understand them is the key to unlocking better relationships.

4. Who is Missing?

During the workday, with so many deadlines driving our behaviors it is easy to omit steps in a process. Sometimes, we even omit key colleagues because we feel hurried.

When discussing big work decisions, noticing who is in the discussions is easy. Noticing who is absent takes thoughtful deliberation, something that is tremendously valuable. It is worth halting processes until the correct stakeholders are present to help contribute critical information and ideas to the discussion. Whether you are creating meetings or attending them, it is worth your time to examine the list of everyone who is included. If it looks like someone was overlooked or omitted, consult with organizers and mention the names of those who need to be in the meeting.

NEED ASSISTANCE?

Do you need more ideas about building or tightening your network? Download a free networking organizer at www.michaelgneece.com. While you are there, you can even set up a free introductory call with me to start planning for your unique situation. Nobody should have to do this alone. You deserve a thriving community who will be with you as you grow your career.

CHAPTER 9
WE BUILD THE FUTURE WE WANT TO LIVE IN

Imagine that over the next few years, we continue to feed into narratives driven by personalities, driven by the concepts of "you're either with us or against us" and a sense that you must pick one side to support and hate the other. Genuine discussion instantly halts when someone declares, "Oh, you're one of those nuts!" When one voice is shut down both parties make no progress and dig deeper into their positions. Everything rides on your group having more power, not better ideas. Everything depends on control. Meanwhile, you and others grow more exasperated, righteously indignant, angry, and disconnected. A war between us and them feels inevitable, and you are exhausted. Will war come? Why do we have to fight it? Will the whole world burn to the ground? All of this means that your workplace becomes a minefield for what topics not

to discuss, full of deep inner turmoil as you see someone crying in the breakroom or missing a lot of work. Was it because
of something in the news?

Now, imagine instead that humankind takes the next three
hundred years to build a future based on compassion, curiosity, and support of each other. Human beings elevate and hon-
or people who work hard and show respect for others. They
mindfully lift each other, especially those who are downtrodden or who feel voiceless. Imagine that these descendants create videos of their lives, their adventures, their struggles, and
their secret methods for "figuring it all out" to send back
through time to give us a roadmap to peace, harmony, progress, and hope.

That is *Star Trek*.

What the unacquainted see when they think of *Star Trek* is
a science fiction television and movie franchise that chronicles
the adventures of future space explorers in search of strange
new worlds and alien civilizations. To those who don't know
the characters and stories, they confuse *Star Trek* with *Star
Wars* and think, "Oh, more space stuff." But diehard *Star Trek*
fans see within it the framework for building a future we want
to live in.

What I adore about *Star Trek*'s 11 television series, 13 movies, and books is this: the only qualification you need to be part
of the club is to be kind. All sentient creatures invented as part
of the *Star Trek* universe—blue aliens, androids, creatures
made of shimmering clouds, holographic people, and humans

of any color, gender, or background—are heard, honored, and respected. So, what exactly is *Star Trek*?

During the American-Soviet cold war era, racial and gender equality struggles exploded into mainstream consciousness in the United States. *Star Trek* creator Gene Roddenberry designed the original television series with characters on the starship Enterprise who looked like the people at the heart of contemporary American struggles. Nichelle Nichols played the part of a communications officer who happened to be Black and female. She worked alongside Walter Koenig, who portrayed a Russian navigator; George Takei, who portrayed a Japanese American helmsman; and Leonard Nimoy, who played the half-human, half-alien science officer. While the Captain, James T. Kirk, portrayed by William Shatner, happened to be a straight, white, American man, these other characters, and the actors who played them, were unusual on mainstream television of the 1960s.

Nichelle Nichols captured the imagination of many Americans through her portrayal of Nyota Uhura, an honored bridge officer among the crew of the starship Enterprise. When Nichols decided to leave the show after a single season and mentioned it to Martin Luther King, Jr. at a fundraising event, he talked her out of leaving the show. "You cannot...Don't you see what this man (Roddenberry) is doing, who has written this? This is the future. He has established us as we should be seen. Three hundred years from now, we are here. We are marching. And, this is the first step. When we see you, we see ourselves, and we see ourselves as intelligent and beautiful and proud." Nichols returned to work that following Monday and instead of quitting, continued with the series through its completion, a follow-up animated series, and six movies.

This optimistic vision of our future is so gripping that there are hundreds of podcasts about various aspects of *Star Trek*, including humanism (*Humanist Trek*), feminism (*Women at Warp: A Star Trek Podcast*), gender preference and gender identity (*Star Trek Discovery Pod*), bioethics, science, technology, the nature of humanity, politics, economics, and space exploration. YouTubers tease apart plotlines of the television series, movies, books, and fan fiction, discussing whether *Star Trek* characters would be Republicans or Democrats, whether a decision made by a *Star Trek* character was ethically sound, and which pets on each series were the best. Millions of *Star Trek* fans analyze what makes this vision of our future so appealing. It is like a vision from the future that we are all trying to inspect and decipher so we know how to get there.

The impact of this unique franchise reverberates in our current society in innumerable ways. Countless scientists and engineers point back to watching *Star Trek* as kids as a reason for seeking out careers that would allow them to emulate the characters in the show and build the technology captured in the series. Doors that open at your grocery store as they detect your presence seem completely normal and standard, but they were inspired by the doors that whooshed open in the mid-1960s *Star Trek* shows. Communicators carried by the

Enterprise crew inspired mobile devices that are must-haves for most adults in the United States. Even the 3-D printers of today act like primitive, early attempts to mimic *Star Trek* replicators that could create meals, clothing, or tools.

Star Trek's typical format of a starship with officers and crew aboard to serve various functions serves perfectly as an analog for companies and corporations as well. Main characters invariably hold vital roles on the ship that align with common work roles at any company in our times. In charge of research and development are Spock, chief engineer Montgomery Scott, and chief medical officer Dr. Leonard McCoy, with the three of them using logic, reason, data collection, their experience and training, and futuristic technologies to innovate everything from new technologies to cures for diseases. Chief Navigator Pavel Chekov pays attention to forces at work on the ship and helps plot a course, much like a marketing expert might help give the best options for strategy at a company. Chief Pilot Hikaru Sulu utilizes the ship's resources to push forward along the preferred path, much like a chief operations officer at a company will ensure that vision is implemented and the company steers in a preferred direction. Chief communications officer Uhura knows how to communicate both with her shipmates and Starfleet—the equivalent of a company headquarters "home office"—as well as with unexpected aliens the crew encounters. The supervisor and leader of the group is Captain Kirk who takes input and expertise from all the others and then makes decisions based on reason and instinct.

These characters have jobs to do in a workplace they all worked hard to be included in, much like you and your colleagues took on education and gained experience that helped you get through interviews and be hired at your workplace. This futuristic workplace carries out the business of each day by asking great questions of each other, assuming high competency and motivation among their colleagues, and investing in knowing each other well enough so that when emergencies come up, a knowing glance or a coded message can easily be understood across all the major characters. Don't we all wish for more curiosity and relationships with our colleagues built on mutual respect?

More modern incarnations of the *Star Trek* universe have included blind engineers, androids who have become sentient and whose rights are vigorously debated; same-sex main characters married to each other in healthy, loving relationships; Black female characters rise to top leadership of their starships; gender-fluid characters are openly celebrated as they create chosen family. There's even a holographic emergency doctor whose program runs so long that he becomes sentient and must grapple with the meaning of existence. These characters' values align with those of future society: curiosity, kindness, empathy, mutual respect, a sense of fairness, and a desire to help those around them, even if the cost is great.

Perhaps Roddenberry studied John Rawls' philosophical arguments pertaining to fairness and justice in a variety of articles Rawls wrote in the 1950s and 1960s. As Roddenberry created *Star Trek* from 1966 to 1968, Rawls was forming and writing about his ideas, including the idea of the Veil of Ignorance, first widely available to the world in his 1971 book *A Theory of Justice*. Simply put, Rawls encourages us to stand behind a Veil of Ignorance as we engage in society-building, stating that if we don't know what position we will hold in that society, we would be wise to make sure all within it are supported and treated fairly, with dignity and kindness.

Regardless of his familiarity with Rawls' early writings, Roddenberry must have understood a similar view of justice and applied those understandings to crafting the universe of *Star Trek*. Not only does it not matter what gender or race you are in the social order of Roddenberry's imagined future, it doesn't matter at all what kind of body you have. It doesn't even matter if you have a physical body at all. After all, if you have kindness, curiosity, a sense of fairness, and a good work ethic, how could it possibly matter how you appear? Tall, short, Black, white, green, metal, gendered, nongendered— these are not the measures of your worth in this future we envision. You have value, you are important, and so are all the other thinking beings around you.

Assuming that the kind of future described above appeals to you as much as it does to me, one in which all people are valued, heard, respected, and honored, then the big question we have to ask ourselves is this: how can we build the future we want to live in?

It is tempting to think one route to pursue might be to

leave all current societies behind, just like pilgrims of old left Europe to come to the New World where they hoped to create Utopia. Yet, when this has been attempted in the past, the very utopian ideals that prompted massive action seem to slip through the cracks.

Perhaps, it is because the voyagers who left their physical surroundings and the constraints of their societies unwittingly dragged their biases, xenophobia, and arrogance with them. The past is riddled with examples of those who seemed to have the best intentions, but all too quickly enjoyed a sense of supremacy over others because of their gender (almost always male), race (mostly Anglo-Saxon white), and religion.

Maybe change doesn't have to be so dramatic after all. Maybe you don't have to move across the world to build a better one. I suggest a humbler and more effective method for building this future: start with yourself and those around you. Be accountable and work to change injustices and inequities you observe wherever you are. As you pursue making the world a better place and building a better future, cultivate allies and followers who see that same vision you see and are willing to work hard to achieve it. Remember, vision alone won't get you there, you'll need to adopt principles you regularly put into action.

To that end, here are the principles that will get us there.

ALWAYS LEAD WITH KINDNESS

Hold close anyone who pays you back in kind, i.e. responding to your kindness with kindness of their own. At work, this means having a network you can rely on, one that you consistently feed with support, kindness, and uplift.

Model kindness even to those who respond to your kindness by trying to take advantage of you, or who treat you with cruelty, belittlement, indifference, or dishonesty. This will do two things: 1) it will help you understand the depth of their untrustworthy or unkind nature; and 2) it will inform you of what shape their toxicity will take so you can determine what measures are needed to avoid those toxic actions and attitudes.

OTHER'S REFLEXIVE ACTIONS ARE PROBABLY NOT AIMED AT YOU

As a rational optimist, I hope for and expect most people will respond to kindness with kindness. I also expect that not everyone will. Every now and again, there will be people who literally or figuratively try to punch me in the face. If you can accept that some people will take a swing at you, you can be ready to step aside to watch the punch drift by while also calmly looking for the exit.

Fully absorb the idea that *hurt people hurt people*. This means that those who have been emotionally or psychologically wounded without healing fully will carry those wounds and inflict pain on others. Genuinely understanding this means that when someone sends you a snarky email or acts rudely to you during a meeting, you can notice their pain and choose not to accept their actions as having anything to do with you at all. Do not take those emotions into yourself as if they were intended for you. This can allow you to feel compassion for their pain and curb your ego's response that would have you punch back. It allows you choice.

As a longtime student of martial arts, my advice is simple: if you recognize when others are about to throw a punch, you can prepare and calmly act. You can avoid the punch or deflect it. Perhaps, you don't even show up for the fight. Recognize your instinct to fight force with force, then act out of compassion instead. While you might want to send an angry reply to an angry email, if you stay calm, you will realize it is better to set up a meeting. In that meeting, they must look you in the eye while you discuss the topic at hand. Be sure to start that discussion with kind inquiries about how they are, how their family is, or familiar positive topics you've discussed in the past. Talk about what shared goals you have and how you are on the same team. Show up prepared with good answers, creative solutions, and a lot of curiosity.

By showing up with an attitude of supportiveness, with a focus on common goals that you state aloud, and interest in that colleague's concerns, your chances of a peaceful resolution increase. You might even get an apology, though that is not the goal. The goal is to have conclusions that make sense, serve a reasonable business purpose, and are not clouded by anyone's temporary emotional state.

If you short-circuit bad behaviors by avoiding and deflecting them instead of fighting back with the same behaviors, you prevent having to apologize for your own behaviors that met someone when they were at their worst. This powerfully places in your hands the potential to avoid missteps of your own while also making others' lives brighter. Using this kindness superpower, you teach a more positive way of interacting. It trains you for the next possible difficult encounter where you will be listening to the hidden subtext of why they behave the way they do. It also establishes your reputation as someone who will always meet others with genuine warmth and kindness. This allows you to become a mentor and role model for others and the opportunity to help colleagues through a difficult season of life. You might even make a friend or two that you didn't expect.

BUILD AN IMMUNITY TO TOXINS

If a repeat-offender colleague hurls toxic behaviors your way consistently, document what they are doing and when they do it using a secure diary or calendar. Involve your supervisor. Consider involving your human resources partners. Try to keep that colleague out of your life as much as possible. There is no reason to tolerate repeated toxic behaviors.

If, along a bumpy path with a colleague, you feel like things are so horrible and unending that you cannot improve them on your own, utilize the strategies above and remind yourself that nothing is ever as bad as you fear nor as good as you hope. Our emotions can convince us that things are bigger than they are and might last longer than they do. Consider mapping out alternatives to sticking around in your current role at your work if you have one or more genuinely toxic colleagues.

ABANDONED PATHS PREPARE YOU FOR NEW ADVENTURES

As you navigate through a career, remember that some jobs will seem, in retrospect, like wrong turns away from a hypothetical better path that got away. Some jobs can feel like they were wasted time. But, those paths were the ones that made you who you are and helped you store away benefits for later that you could not guess when you started. Here is an example of what I mean:

As a high school student, I started taekwondo and hungrily attended every class I could. I practiced at home constantly, so I rose through the ranks quickly. By the time I was in my early college career, I was an instructor at the local dojo, teaching others how to kick, punch, and block. I loved the sense of accomplishment and how confident and healthy it made me feel. I enjoyed it so much that I even considered becoming a full-time martial arts instructor as my profession.

That idea never panned out because I chose other paths aligned with my other commitments and interests, such as my paid job giving planetarium shows at Morehead Planetarium on UNC's campus. I also felt my classwork in physics might lead to other careers. My taekwondo side path could have been my central path, but I chose otherwise. Did guessing at my future cause me anxiety? Yes. Was I cutting off other paths by selecting a singular path in the moment? Without a doubt. Were the paths I was cutting away worthless? Of course not.

By learning and teaching taekwondo, I gained the benefits of becoming aware of my surroundings, learning how to defend myself, and keeping my body healthy and lean. The hidden benefits, however, took longer to identify. Specifically, I love teaching others and got lots of practice. I learned customer service by helping parents sign their kids up for classes and helping martial arts students select proper defensive gear. By teaching taekwondo, I also began to understand spatial relationships, force and motion, and other physics concepts that were helpful in earning my bachelor's degree in physics.

I no longer teach martial arts, but what if I had filled that time another way? If I had stayed home watching TV, I would not have grown in the same way. By leading students through kicking and punching exercises, I touched the lives of everyone I taught, gained skills, enhanced myself, and stayed in motion.

When my son and I decided to hike the Appalachian Trail together during the first summer of the COVID-19 pandemic, we didn't know if it was "the right choice" to make. As finite human beings with no ability to know with certainty what the future holds, who knows what the right choices could be? We are always making good guesses about our intended actions with no guarantee of outcomes. We might have stacked the odds in our favor, or taken a risky chance, but that is always the best we can do.

So, we chose to hike in June and decided to add a third hiker to the troop. Our packs were heavy with gear we thought we would need, but that also made the hiking more difficult. We added a charity fundraiser and made the hike more about others and less about ourselves.

None of those finer details mattered.

What mattered was that we made decisions and moved forward. Each decision felt reasonable, like it would enhance the adventure, help us or others, and keep risks at bay. Did things go wrong? As we sprinted over the crest of a mountain through fog, pelting rain, and lightning, we sure thought so! Did we adjust and still have a memorable and worthwhile, amazing adventure? Absolutely.

In spite of rain-proof maps and a GPS that occasionally worked on our mobile devices, we still got lost. The best thing about going down a wrong path is that you can triangulate. Look back along the path you took, look at where you want to go, and then determine what's next. You evaluate every couple of miles, or even every couple of steps, if you need to keep going on the current path or divert to a better one. If you end up backtracking to take a different path you neglected before, it is because you gained knowledge from the original imperfect path where you could go next.

As you implement your efforts to make a positive impact on the world, focus on your inner compass. You know right from wrong, what you believe, and what actions are most likely to make the world better. Regardless of the terrain you encounter, stay in motion always calibrated by that compass. Stay hydrated and take breaks, but do not get stuck in one place wishing for another life without taking action. Move forward, compare your location on your current path to other locations on possible paths, determine the best way forward, and keep going.

When you feel really stuck, like things are bad for you and there is no hope and you just wish someone would come and help, remember this quote from Winston Churchill: "If you're going through hell, keep going." More importantly, reach out to your network of friends and supporters who will be there to walk alongside you.

Even along abandoned paths, you pick up skills, friends, and perspectives. You discover what you want and what you don't want. Those experiences become stories about your origin. They become career paths you can tell others to try if you think it might fit them better, or maybe they become cautionary tales to junior colleagues you coach one day.

ACT. DO IT NOW. GET GOING.

If you want things to happen, start doing the work. If you stand in one spot, the world consistently appears a certain way to you. If you move a few paces, even down a not-great path, you can at least triangulate to see if there is a better path and then adjust to get onto it. Standing still literally gets you nowhere.

If you ever feel hesitant to start moving in one direction, remember that making no decision is misleading. It is really a decision to remain motionless and, therefore, not experience possibilities. You are deciding to stay stuck. Don't pretend otherwise, and don't lie to the rest of us. Get moving.

As long as you keep your beliefs, values, short-term and long-term goals clear as you make decisions about where to apply your energy and skills, every small step forward propels you. When they add up, you'll be miles from where you started. Basketball legend Michael Jordan once said as advice on giving things a try: "You miss 100% of the shots you don't take." The more shots you take, the more times you will figuratively score points in your own personal game of life. Standing and staring at the basket while never taking a single shot gains you nothing. Go take some shots!

TOOLS AND TAKEAWAYS

Life Pursuits Exercise:

1. Set a timer for 20 minutes. List out everything you think is most important in your life. You are answering the question: where should I spend my time?

    - List things that inspire you, bring you joy, pull you into a state of flow when you do them. Perhaps it is math, spending time with animals, or building model airplanes. There are no wrong answers, just answers that fit versus answers that don't.

2. Circle the top five items from your list.

3. Look those top five items over and ponder them hard. Will these help build the future you want to live in? Are these skills you can apply? Will they enhance your life? Will they get you to a version of yourself you are proud of?

If you have an inkling that others might dismiss anything on your list, remember that this is your list and not theirs. Besides, if you think you can change the world through art, grooming cats, balancing financial statements, repairing plumbing, writing short stories, or some other pursuit that appeals to you, you are most likely correct. You may not even see it yourself as you ponder this list, but if you think creatively, it could come after years of effort and skill-building.

The third and final step is to select the top choice out of

those five. This is the item you want to start on first. It might be the best, it might just be the most appealing for where you are in life right now, but whatever made you select it, trust that instinct.

Since this feels like your most important item, create repeating times on your calendar when you will focus on it. Make the time for it early in the day whenever you can so that you are at your most energetic with your best focus, and when few demands of daily life have taken over your attention. As Oliver Burkeman advises in *4000 Weeks: Time Management for Mortals*, "the advice given in the financial world to pay yourself first else the money will vanish as you pay for other things in the meantime, the same applies to your time. If you do not set aside your time early and often, so, too, will it vanish."

In other words, if you wait until the end of daily tasks to try to fit in your most important goal, you will reflect on your activities over the course of months or even years and find that you have devoted little or no time to the endeavor you claim is so important.

After placing your top item on your calendar, go through the other four pursuits you see value in and do the same. Once they are on the calendar, set one more calendar entry that is monthly titled "Check in." It can be 30 minutes long or more. This is the time where you scan back through the calendar and evaluate how it is going. Honestly evaluate how much you adhered to each effort, and determine if you need more time on one and less on another and if you included an item that doesn't feel so important after all. If you left something important out, add it. These honest evaluations inform you so you can create the results you want.

Stick With It!

It can be easy to cut an activity because it suddenly became complicated, felt frustrating, or took more time than you would have liked. Those are terrible reasons to eliminate that activity. Sometimes being frustrated and feeling overwhelmed means you are in a creative process that you need to keep working through. Other times, it might mean you need to take a step back, let your brain process what's going on, and return to the activity. It might mean that you need something to assist you with what you are working on; perhaps an ally or two, or a training course, or the perspective of a mentor you can check in with periodically. Abandoning a cherished activity because it became hard makes no sense when you realize that any endeavor you will ever try that has value to it will require effort and become difficult at moments.

Lives Have Seasons

Much like there are seasons in a year, each one better for certain activities than others, there are also seasons in our lives. For a few months or a few years, you will find that a particular pursuit makes sense and feels right. During that time, other activities simply may not appeal. Trust your instincts.

Think of classes in college, how they only last for a few months then you move on to other classes during the next term. Life after college can have similar time periods of weeks, months, or years.

How can you tell?

Trust your instincts. That is probably the best indicator of what you feel you are ready for and what you genuinely want.

If you want reassurance, talk to your mentor or a trusted friend.

Regardless, if you decide not to pursue something you genuinely care about for a few months or a few years, practice patience with yourself. Know that for most activities, stopping for a while does not mean you have shut the door to that activity forever.

When I was sixteen, I spent the summer working as a student assistant in the free electron laser lab at Duke University. When you add that experience to my bachelor's degree in physics from UNC, it could seem like my life would be spent working on physics equations in a classroom or lab for the rest of my life. It turns out, however, that I am not suited to work in experimental physics. It is not something I particularly enjoy nor have patience for. I might not have enough talent for it either, but I will never know because I don't care to invest my time in it. A quick aside: not knowing if my mental capacity could keep up with the physics classes bothered me for many years. It felt like a failure. There was this nagging voice in my head telling me I didn't "stick it out" and "stay tough." I finally figured out that nobody was keeping score except me. Just because I hold scientists in high esteem doesn't mean I failed by pursuing activities apart from science. Even astrophysicists think there are smarter people.

Why should interests and talents be agonizing? I have others that feel like a celebration for investing my time and resources in. I cannot do it all in this one and only lifetime, so why would I spend time doing anything that made me feel miserable? Why not choose something I am excited about?

Pursuing physics for a lifetime just so I could brag about how I showed fortitude, endurance, and the ability to ignore my own misery would be ridiculous. But, as a side-quest that taught me a lot about who I am, it was worth it. I feel great that I went through that interesting and difficult summer job. I love that I earned an undergraduate degree in physics. Those experiences set me up to pursue science communication as a planetarium show presenter, allowed me to understand the best way to break a wooden board with my bare hands in taekwondo, and gave me a thousand other benefits besides, not least of all that I can and will choose happiness—which makes me kinder.

When you recognize that a path in your life is one that you should backtrack on after having given it a solid effort, just backtrack with a smile on your face knowing that a better path awaits. Go make the world a better place with your other talents and leave the self-imposed suffering behind! You'll be kinder too.

Volunteerism:

You will have free time beyond working on your hobbies and career. During these open moments in your life, you can make a direct difference in the world by volunteering at a soup kitchen, animal shelter, or in innumerable other future-building uplifting pursuits.

Whether at work or in your community, you can find volunteer opportunities that help shape others' lives. As I mentioned in the last chapter, fundraising for various good causes such as fighting homelessness or food insecurity can be quite easy. Choose to volunteer for the Red Cross, Feeding America, or Habitat for Humanity.

1. Select one or two charitable activities or organizations aligned with your interests and beliefs.

2. Find a volunteer buddy! Most workplaces have charitable efforts for donating to a cause or giving time to an organization. Colleagues frequently make great volunteer buddies.

3. Decide how often you want to volunteer. Weekly, monthly, and quarterly volunteering is common.

4. Create calendar entries for volunteer activities aligned with what you find available that aligns with your preferences, buddies, and frequency.

5. Add one extra calendar entry that recurs quarterly reminding you to refresh your calendar with new events.

Special Projects:

I invite you to make other impacts on the world, asking you to join me in my own endeavors. I write, I create communities at my work and in my industry, and I give talks around the globe.

Be bold and decide how you can influence the world by creating uplift in ways unique to you. You could write, make video content, create visual artwork, or otherwise contribute to the beauty of the world.

Consider those unique talents you have and brainstorm how to grow those over the coming years and decades. How could you make a bigger difference to marginalized communities? What can you do to improve society? How can you stand up for justice by employing those skills?

NEED ASSISTANCE?

How can you start building the future you want to live in? Go to www.michaelgneece.com and tap into the suggestions on the "Building Our Future Together" page. While you are there, schedule a free "Future Building" call with me and let's get started!

Made in United States
North Haven, CT
31 January 2024

48163938R00124